World University Library

The World University Library is an international series
of books, each of which has been specially commissioned.
The authors are leading scientists and scholars from all over
the world who, in an age of increasing specialisation, see the
need for a broad, up-to-date presentation of their subject.
The aim is to provide authoritative introductory books for
students which will be of interest also to the general reader.
The series is published in Britain, France, Germany,
Holland, Italy, Spain, Sweden and the United States.

E. A. Wrigley

Population and History

World University Library

McGraw-Hill Book Company
New York Toronto

To my wife

© E. A. Wrigley 1969
Reprinted 1976
Reprinted 1979
Library of Congress Catalog Card Number: 68–13142
Phototypeset by BAS Printers Limited, Wallop, Hampshire, England
Manufactured by LIBREX, Milan, Italy

Contents

In the diagrams red represents fertility and green represents mortality throughout.

1 Historical demography

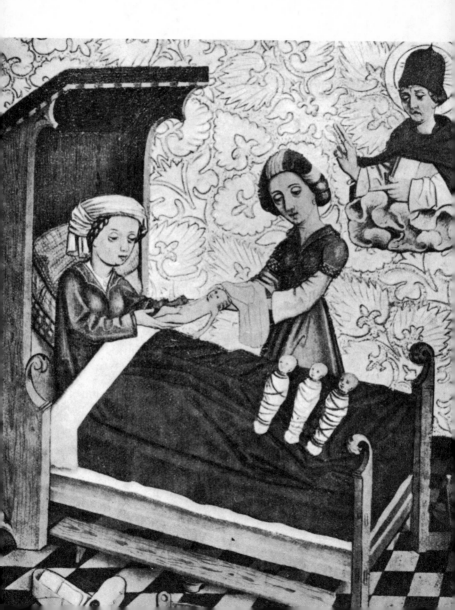

1 Historical demography

Population characteristics

When Kant wished to illustrate the notion that even historical events whose occurrence seems quite random and unpredictable may in the mass show notable regularities, he turned to population.[1] Whereas it would be hazardous indeed to predict the day of any one man's death, or the date of a young girl's marriage and the dates on which she will give birth to children, for any thousand men or young girls much more confident predictions can be made. In studying the characteristics of large populations patterns are found. Women are not equally likely to marry at all ages: nor are men equally likely to die at all times of life.

Some of the regularities which are revealed by the study of populations are found in all societies and persist even in cases which at first sight seem very different. For example, it is probably true of all societies that the first few hours of a baby's life are those in which the risk of death is greatest, that the risk declines from birth, rapidly at first and then very slowly, to reach a minimum usually in the early teens. Thereafter the danger of dying for each unit of time lived rises with increasing rapidity as the years pass. The shape, therefore, of any one schedule of mortality by age will have much in common with any other, though its level may be such as to mean an expectation of life at birth as low as 20 years or as high as 75 (see figure 1·1).

Knowledge of regularities of this type enables governments today accurately to forecast many needs. For example, the number of school leavers entering the labour force ten years hence can be calculated with only small margins of doubt from the number of young children today. Ignorance of these regularities sometimes led governments in the past into errors which now appear comical. When Kant was a young man, for instance, the British government granted Exchequer life annuities without distinction of age or sex to help to attract loans. As a result the Exchequer lost money, for many shrewd speculators (mostly Dutchmen) took out annuities on behalf of young girls whose expectation of life was far too good for

Figure 1·1 Age-specific mortality rates (per 1000)
where expectation of life is 30 and 70 years.
The shapes of the curves are similar
in spite of the very different absolute rates.[2]
The vertical scale is logarithmic.

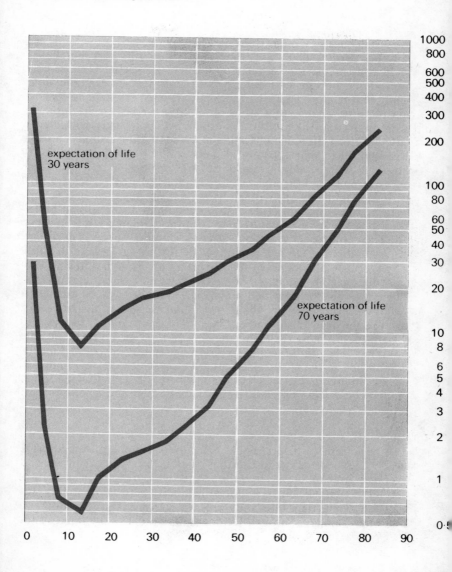

the Exchequer's accounts to balance.[3]

Other aspects of demographic behaviour, on the other hand, show only regularities peculiar to particular societies because customs differ. Few generalisations about marriage, for example, hold good universally. There are societies in which a man is free to marry any woman except a few of his closest relatives, his mother, sister, aunt, daughter, niece. In others his choice may be severely circumscribed. In much of India until recently, for instance, a man was obliged to marry within his subcaste but was debarred from marriage with a wide group of kin having in common a distant ancestor reckoned through the father's line. Moreover, he was not permitted to marry any woman living in his own village or a neighbouring one: and still other restrictions might also apply to him.[4] In some societies it is almost unknown for a woman not to marry, and marry moreover at or soon after the onset of puberty; in others large numbers of women remain single for life (in Ireland in 1901 22 per cent of all women in the age-group 45–54 were still single).[5] In some societies a man may take only one wife; in others several. There are societies in which a marriage can normally be dissolved only by death; others in which the mutual consent of the partners, or even the decision of one partner, can bring a match to an end. Where the average age of marriage is as high as 30, rare but not unknown, even those women who do marry must expect to spend half of their fertile life in social situations in which they are unlikely to have intercourse or bear children. Where it is as low as the teens many women will bear children throughout their fertile period.

The family

The basic unit of demographic behaviour is the family, the most nearly universal of all institutions. The measures used by demographers are all built up from events which occur in a family setting. Almost all births and deaths modify an existing family. In the case of marriages not only are two existing families modified, but a new family is formed. Demography measures the timing and number of these family events and the structure of the populations in which they take place. But the family is also a basic unit of social activity generally. Most children pass their formative years in a family, learning there those forms of conduct, values and attitudes of mind which make the continuation of society possible. The process of socialisation is very largely a family matter, and the study of family structure and relationships sheds much light on the behaviour of society at large. Demography and the study of society, therefore, whether in the present or the past, have many points of contact. And there are equally close ties between the demographic characteristics and the economic fortunes and structures of societies. The historical demography of communities forms a nexus linking together so many aspects of their life that its study is an excellent point of departure for the study of social and economic function and change generally.

In spite of the occasional ambiguity which the use of the term family is apt to produce (see pages 28–9), it is an exceptionally convenient unit of study. Naturally this is true of the analysis of the circumstances of individual families, but it is also true when studying larger units because families can be grouped together like building blocks into larger structures. As the topic studied changes in scale, from family to village or occupational group, and from these in turn to class, nation or continent, so the types of interrelationships which can be laid bare with a demographic scalpel also change. This flexibility is both convenient and important. It makes it possible either to follow out on the large scale, say, the correlation between fluctuations in the price of wheat and mortality rates over a large region, or to examine the effects of serious harvest failures within individual families. If, for example, a fifth of the population of a group of parishes died from undernourishment and disease in the wake of successive bad harvests, this illustrates the intimate connection in pre-industrial times between the fortunes of harvest, the price of bread and the scale of mortality. But it is also interesting to know how individual families were affected, for deaths were not spread evenly through all the families then living, each losing one or two of its members. Instead the typical pattern was that deaths were heavily concentrated amongst a fraction only of the families, those which were unlucky enough to lose their main breadwinner or which were exposed by chance to infection. Or mortality may prove to have been especially marked in particular areas or among certain social or economic groups. Each great event can be broken down into smaller issues, and each of these examined at the appropriate scale.

Historical demography deals with all men and women, not simply those who were powerful, well-born, wealthy or literate. By analysing parish registers, listings of inhabitants, returns made to census authorities and the like, we can look into the lives of ordinary people in the past, comparing peasant with gentleman, miner with clothmaker, countryman with city dweller, and so on. Where the necessary records are preserved there is a chance to get down to the roots of society almost as a social anthropologist tries to gain an insight into a contemporary community by listening to its members tell of the great events of their lives, of birth, marriage and death and the cluster of social attitudes, customs and sanctions which relate to them. The parish registers and other local documents can often provide eloquent witness to the effects on the lives of ordinary people of local economic or social conditions even though no dialogue with the dead is possible.

Birth, death and marriage rates form the basic descriptive language of historical demography. Paradoxically, there is often more complete and reliable quantitative information to be had about birth, death and marriage in the past than about prices or production. The intimate events of family life round the hearth are better recorded than the affairs of the market place. Marital fertility is sometimes easier to discover than the price of grain; statistics of illegitimacy than those of smuggling. The fact that it can provide quantitative measures of events in the past is one of the most valuable attributes of historical demography. It gives statistical backbone to inquiries which badly need it. To say that child mortality was appallingly high in pre-industrial times, or that families were large, is to make a statement which is implicitly statistical and which can be supported or disproved from suitable sources using appropriate techniques. Too often generalisations of this type are largely dependent on literary evidence, or based on untypical groups in the population.

Sometimes the results of more painstaking inquiries do not support earlier notions. It is clear, for example, that the conjugal family, consisting of father, mother and children only, so often held to be the result of industrialisation and urban living, was normal in much of western Europe for several centuries before the industrial revolution. The extended family, with three generations and two or more married couples in a single large household, was not a universal pre-industrial phenomenon. Again, it is not true that fertility and mortality in pre-industrial societies were uniformly high. Nor did girls always marry young. Indeed women in Elizabethan England probably married two or three years later on an average than they do in England today. When accurate quantitative information has been obtained it is a great stimulus to further inquiry and reflection. To learn, for example, that there was at a certain period a significant rise in the average age at which women married may prove a valuable clue to other changes going on in the community – perhaps a change in inheritance customs making it more difficult for men to acquire a holding and so to marry young; perhaps a reduction in employment opportunities; or a change in the status of women. In addition there will probably be direct demographic consequences, notably a fall in the average number of children born to each couple.

The wider value of demographic studies lies in the sensitivity with which a community's demography reflected its economic, social and natural environments. These relationships were two-way. Fertility and mortality were not simply a passive reflection of the general circumstances of a community. They helped in turn to shape those circumstances.

Before turning to the populations of particular places and periods in a wider setting, however, we must first look at the interplay between purely demographic variables and consider some simple models of the general relationships between population characteristics and economic and social conditions. It is important to know, for example, how a change in fertility may affect the age structure of a community, or what effect an increasing density of population may be expected to have upon death rates in pre-industrial societies. It is also important to appreciate the limitations of all models and especially to understand how a change in the material technology of a society can transform the inter-relationships between demography, economy and society. The rest of this chapter and the next are largely given over to these questions. Because of limitations of space, some topics both in the first two chapters and later are touched on only *en passant* in spite of their great importance. This is notably true, for example, of migration.

Varieties of demographic equilibrium

Fertility and mortality levels may each vary widely, and this has always been so. The average size of families may be as high as ten or as low as two. Expectation of life may be as high as 75 years or as low as 20. Even before the changes of the last hundred years which have greatly increased the spread of possibilities, a striking variety of birth and death rates could be found. But it does not follow from this that all possible combinations of the two are equally likely to occur in practice. Indeed, only a rather restricted range of combinations occurred over long periods in the past, and it seems safe to assert that any drastic imbalance between fertility and mortality can only be found in any society over a small number of generations.

Very high fertility associated with low mortality, to take an extreme case, may cause populations to double every 20 years or so. This implies a rate of increase of just over three per cent a year and would produce a thousandfold increase in two centuries. It will very soon lead to a 'standing room only' situation, while the reverse of this will soon bring extinction by natural decrease. Both types of extreme situation may occasionally be found for short periods but

Figure 1·2 A negative feedback situation in which an increase in fertility provokes changes which tend to keep population numbers close to their original level.

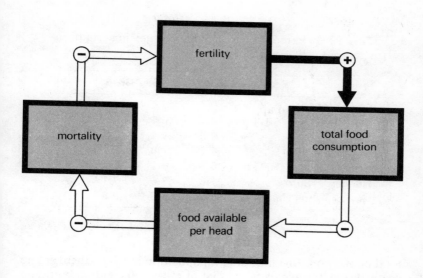

the normal position was one in which fertility and mortality were in rough balance with each other. In most pre-industrial societies indeed population characteristics tended to be self-balancing, any change in one aspect of the society's demography tending to produce changes elsewhere which counterbalanced the original change. The diagram figure 1·2 shows, for instance, how an increase in fertility may produce a countervailing rise in mortality as the pressure is intensified upon the food supplies of the area and its resource base generally. The rising death rates will in turn cause a higher proportion of marriages to be interrupted by the death of one or other partner before the end of the wife's fertile period and thus further offset the original fertility rise.

An equilibrium between births and deaths, can, of course arise in many different ways. It may be helpful to consider two extreme cases in order to bring home the range of possible combinations of fertility, mortality and nuptiality which will produce an unchanging

Table 1·1 Percentages of single women in certain
five-year age-groups.[6]

	35–9	40–4	45–9	50–4
France (1962)	10·4	9·1	9·2	9·1
West Germany (1961)	12·7	10·8	9·3	9·6
Sweden (1960)	9·8	9·4	10·9	13·8
Denmark (1960)	8·3	7·8	9·1	11·4
Czechoslovakia (1961)	6·5	6·1	6·0	6·9
Hungary (1960)	7·6	7·5	7·1	7·4
New Zealand (1961)	7·7	6·8	8·6	9·7

total population. Imagine, first, a population in which there are no deaths below the age of 50, so that of every 100 children born in a given year all are still living 50 years later; in which all men and women marry; and in which the average number of children born to each couple is 2·00. In these circumstances for every 100 adults in any one generation there must always be the same number in the next.

Needless to say two of the three assumptions about this model population are unreal. There will always be some wastage of life between birth and the age of 50 from congenital defects, from disease and from accidents. And there are always some men and women in each generation who do not marry either from lack of inclination or lack of opportunity (in a population with no deaths before 50 the imbalance of the sexes at birth when there are about 105 boys born for every 100 girls would be preserved throughout the child-bearing period and would probably cause some men to remain bachelors all their lives). Nevertheless, although the state of affairs just supposed will never come about, it has been approached quite closely in recent years in some advanced industrial countries. In these countries the loss of life between birth and the end of the child-bearing period is now slight (for example, in Sweden 943 out of every 1,000 live-born girls would reach the age of 50 at the death rates prevailing in 1959; and 913 out of every 1,000 boys).[7] And the great majority of men and women now marry (see table 1·1).

Since this is so an average family size of only a little more than 2·00 is sufficient to maintain population at its present level in advanced countries. In England an average completed family size of about 2·25 will suffice to achieve this. If average family size in these circumstances is as high as, say, 3·00 children per family, the next generation will be larger than the present in the ratio of 3·00: 2·25, or a third larger. This in turn means that population will increase about two-and-a-half times in a century. Even an average family size of 2·50 is still much more than sufficient to maintain numbers and will give rise over a century to a growth in numbers of well over a third. Since, if present trends continue, the level of mortality in the early decades of life is likely to show a further slight fall in the years to come, and the proportion of women never marrying is also likely if anything to fall, the family size which will ensure that the next generation is as large as the present must also grow smaller.

To bear only two children in the course of the fertile period is, of course, to make use of only a fraction of the reproductive potential of most women. At the other extreme from the case just discussed, therefore, must be envisaged societies in which women bear four or five times as many children on an average. For the married women of any community to bear as many as eight or ten children on an average is rare, though not unknown. In the Hutterite communities in the United States, for example, the average number of live children ever born to married women aged 45–54 in 1950 was 10·6. A still higher extreme was reached by women married at the young age of 18 in the decade 1931–40. Their average completed family size was estimated in 1953 to be likely to be 12·3.[8] But five, six, or seven is a common average completed size for families in pre-industrial societies, and even at this much lower level of fertility it may seem puzzling that populations failed to increase or increased only very slowly. Another hypothetical case may make the situation clearer.

In the first case considered, which we may call population **1**, every 2,000 adults form 1,000 marriages and produce 2,000 children. Birth intervals mean little in a population of this sort since the size of the family is determined to a large extent by the conscious decision of parents and the final size of the family is not closely related to the length of the intervals between births. Any particular couple may in principle decide to have, say, three children and may spread them over five or fifteen years as their individual wishes and circumstances may dictate, though in practice they are likely to have them quite close together early in their marriage.

In the second model population (population **2**) we will suppose that fertility is not the subject of individual choice, though it may be strongly affected by such social customs as the normal length of breast feeding or restrictions on intercourse following the birth of a child. In such a situation the average birth interval is of great importance and serves to determine the general level of fertility of couples once they are married. In this instance suppose that births are spaced out at two-and-a-half year intervals except for the last, so that a woman marrying at the age of 20 and surviving in marriage to the end of her child-bearing life may expect to bear seven or eight children (in arriving at this average family size one may assume that the last birth interval is half as long again as the earlier birth intervals, and that the last child is born when the mother's age is 40: both these were common features of European pre-industrial populations). How then is it in such a population that one generation may be no larger than its predecessor?

Imagine again a group of 2,000 adults representing a cross-section of a larger population. In population **1** there were 1,000 marriages in this population since every adult married. In population **2** we will suppose that ten per cent of this number never marry. This immediately cuts the total possible number of births by ten per cent also

Table 1·2 Three model populations

	1	2	3
Population at age 26 (men and women equal in number)	2,000	2,000	2,000
Number of marriages contracted	1,000	900	1,000
Total births*	2,000	3,780	5,250
Infant deaths	0	880†	0
Number surviving to age 1	2,000	2,900	5,250
Child and young adult deaths 1–25	0	900‡	0
	2,000	2,000	5,250

* 1,000 × 2·00; 900 × 4·20; and 1,000 × 5·25.
† Infant mortality at 275 per 1,000.
‡ This figure agrees closely with a figure calculated from the UN specimen life table for expectation of life at birth of 32·5 years.

(illegitimate births may be ignored for the sake of simple exposition). Secondly, the mean age at first marriage for women may be set at 26 and we will assume further that all brides and grooms married at that age. This is now a very important statistic since the final family size will be largely a function of age at marriage given that there is no deliberate limitation of family size. Such an age at marriage implies an average completed family size of about 5·25 children, a figure less than 70 per cent as large as that which would be reached if women married at 20 rather than 26. But even the figure of 5·25 children per marriage will only be attained if all the marriages contracted are uninterrupted by the death of either spouse until after the end of the wife's child-bearing period. This assumption is written into the first model but is, of course, quite unrealistic for any pre-industrial population. The effect of adult mortality may well be sufficient to reduce the size of families by a fifth or more, say from 5·25 to 4·20 (remarriage of widows and widowers complicates the picture but does not greatly affect the argument).

At this point it is interesting to contrast the number of children produced with the number potentially available if marriage were universal and the mortality conditions were those embodied in the first model (see population **3** in table 1·2). The contrast between potential and performance is already very striking but the total of live births produced by population **2** is nevertheless 3,780, only 72 per cent of the figure for **3,** but still almost twice the number of adults. However, before any one generation can succeed its predecessor and in turn begin to bear children it must first survive the perils of infancy, childhood and adolescence. In a population of this type there will in all probability be a high infant mortality, say at the rate of 275 per 1,000 (infant mortality comprises all deaths occurring before the baby attains its first birthday). This reduces the cohort (the jargon for a generation) of live-born children from 3,780 to about 2,900. It is in keeping with life tables reflecting mortality at this level that the subsequent deaths in childhood and adolescence should reduce this number by a further 900 or so, thus producing in the next generation a population no larger than the previous one.

These examples, incidentally, may be used to show the meaning of two terms which it is often convenient to use in discussions of this type – net and gross reproduction rates. Both are normally based on the experience of women only. A female net reproduction rate measures the number of daughters who would be born to a group of girl babies by the end of their child-bearing period assuming that current age-specific fertility and mortality rates continued unchanged. Thus population **1** in table 1·2 has a NRR of 1·00 because no one dies before the end of the child-bearing period and each woman bears one girl child on an average. The NRR of population **2** is also 1·00 because any 1,000 girl babies are so much reduced by wastage before they reach marriageable age and continued mortality thereafter that, in spite of their high fertility in marriage, they will bear only 1,000 girl children in all (in the table the 3,780 birth population is reduced to 2,000 by age 26 and produces a total of 3,780 births in its turn, a half of each total being females). A NRR of 1·00 implies that in the long term population will remain stable, each generation exactly reproducing itself.

The gross reproduction rate differs from the net in ignoring mortality. In the case of population **1** the GRR, like the NRR is unity or 1·00 (there are no deaths to ignore in this population before the end of the child-bearing period). But population **2** has a GRR of 2·36. Of any 1,000 baby girls, 900 will marry and will bear 4,725 children (900 × 5·25). Half of these will be girls; and thus we get $\frac{4,725}{2 \times 1,000} = 2\cdot36$ (more accurate NRRs and GRRs can be calcuated by adjusting the rates to take account of the imbalance of the sexes at birth). The difference between the GRR and NRR (2·36 and 1·00) is a measure of the throttling back of fertility which occurs wherever death rates are high among children and young adults.

All these models are crude. They are meant to do no more than show how the interplay of the chief demographic variables may produce a general balance between births and deaths, or may cause numbers to rise or fall if their values are slightly altered. It will be clear from population **2** of table 1·2 that many different combinations of characteristics can produce an overall balance between births and deaths. For example, the average age at first marriage for women may be much lower, say 18 or less, as in most Asiatic and African populations.

This immediately greatly increases the completed family size which might at first sight be expected. But some of the other variables may also be different in such a population so that numbers do not rise in spite of the early entry of women into marriage. The fact that more years must be lived in marriage before the child-bearing period is passed makes it more likely that the union will be interrupted by the death of one of the partners, and so increases the proportion of possible births lost, particularly if adult mortality rates are also higher (at a rough calculation this might mean replacing 900 × 4·20 by 900 × 5·70 in population **2** of table 1·2). This compensating tendency will be much strengthened if longer suckling periods, less frequent intercourse, or a higher pregnancy wastage through miscarriage and abortion, increase the average interval between live births. If the average interval were 40 months instead of 30, this, combined with the other changes just posited, would bring average family size back to the level of population **2**.

Or the same effect may be produced in other ways. The average age at which women bear their last child may be lower. Their mean age when the last child was born in populations apparently practising little or no control of conception has been known to range from 43·8 years in early eighteenth century Canada at one extreme down to 27·7 years in the Caribbean area in recent decades.[9] Or infant mortality may be higher; and so on. A rough stability in numbers can thus arise out of many different sets of demographic characteristics. Populations in the past grew very little if at all over long periods of time, and so their demography can often be understood in terms of a model like population **2** in table 1·2. But the absolute level of numbers at which this stability is maintained may nevertheless vary widely. This is very important and interlocks with much else in the social and economic circumstances of each period. It will be examined in some detail in the next chapter.

A further point about population **2** is worth noting. It contains a large reservoir of what might be called frustrated fertility – potential fertility which cannot be realised because mortality is high. If this situation is compared with that of population **3** it is immediately clear how quickly population pressure may build up in a country which passes abruptly from the sort of mortality conditions embodied in population **2** to those of population **1** or **3**. The difference between the GRR and NRR of population **2** is a more exact measure of the same thing. The change comes about not only because a big fall in infant and child mortality may almost double the number of children surviving to maturity from a given cohort of live offspring, but also because when adult mortality is sharply reduced the loss of potential fertility caused by the early end of many marriages is avoided. Thus it is that in the developing countries today there may be both a great fall in mortality and a rise in fertility. The rise in fertility will be compounded if better hygiene and nutrition reduce pregnancy wastage and, by improving the general health of the mother, increase chances of conception.

The age structure of populations

Before dispensing with the model populations of table 1·2, one further general issue may conveniently be dealt with. The fertility and mortality schedules of a population determine its age structure. It can be shown that any combination of fertility and mortality will give rise to a population whose age structure is stable (that is to say one in which the percentage of the total population in any given age-group will not vary provided that fertility and mortality rates do not alter). But if the initial age structure of the population is well removed from the age structure implied by its current fertility and mortality it may then, of course, take several generations for the ultimate age structure to emerge.

A stable population will only rarely also be a stationary population of unchanging total number if fertility and mortality schedules are combined at random. But in all pre-industrial populations there were long periods in which population totals did not change very much. These populations were often both close to stability in the demographic sense and nearly stationary in number, like population 2. And population 1 illustrates the same point for a hypothetical 'modern' population. The age structure of these two stationary populations, however, is quite different.

Figure 1·3 shows the population pyramids of the two populations. In population 1 it was assumed that no deaths occurred below the age of 50. There is therefore no shrinkage in the width of the pyramid below that age. Above it the rate of shrinkage reflects the mortality experience of the healthiest countries today. In population 2 the size of the starting population in relation to the population at age 26 is fixed at 3,780 to 2,000. Infant mortality is also specified and with these aspects of mortality given specimen life tables may be used to complete the rest of the pyramid in a plausible fashion. The pyramid based on population 1 represents, of course, an age distribution which can never be found in reality since there will always be some wastage of life in each age-group through which any cohort of individuals passes, but exaggeration,

Figure 1·3 Age pyramids of two stationary populations with very different fertility and mortality characteristics.
Figure 1·4 Age pyramids of the populations of Hungary (1963), Sweden (1963), Guyana (1960) and Syria (1960).[10] The age pyramids of the model populations of figure 1·3 are also given for comparison. The two sexes are not differentiated.

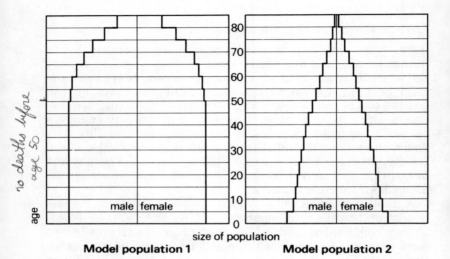

no deaths before age 50

Model population 1　　　　　　　　　　**Model population 2**

here as elsewhere, is often a valuable way of driving a point home.

Figure 1·4 shows that contrasts in age distribution quite as remarkable as those in figure 1·3 occur in reality, though these are not stable populations but rather populations in which either fertility or mortality or both have changed very markedly in recent decades. Moreover in both Guyana and Syria population is growing very rapidly.

That differences in the age structure of populations are very important hardly needs stressing. If we assume, for example, that only those between the age of 15 and 59 are able to contribute to the production of wealth in a country, a ratio of dependents to producers can easily be calculated. In some contemporary populations which have changing fertility and mortality this ratio can fluctuate considerably. It was recently shown, for example, that different assumptions about population change in India might produce a ratio as low as 1·24 or as high as 1·71 in 1986 (the ratios were

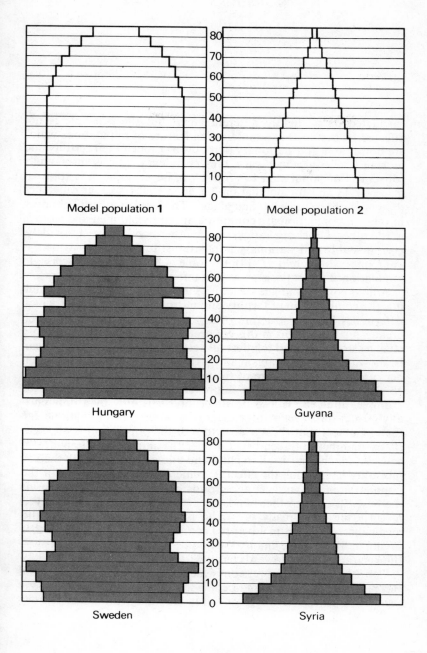

Model population **1**

Model population **2**

Hungary

Guyana

Sweden

Syria

calculated on a slightly different basis, but the principle is not affected by this).[11] It is an interesting feature of populations which are both stable and stationary that however much their fertility and mortality schedules may vary, the dependency ratio is surprisingly constant. For population 1 in figure 1·3, for example, it is approximately 1·43 and for population 2 1·56, a much smaller difference than might be expected at first glance. The large number of children in the one population are counterbalanced by old men and women in the other. Other age ratios, on the other hand, may vary widely, even in stable and stationary populations. In population 1 there is only one schoolchild (5–14) to some 4·46 adult producers; in population 2 the ratio is as low as one to 3·15.

A final point about age structure should also be noted. Although it is the combination of fertility and mortality characteristics which determines the age structure of a population, fertility is of much greater relative weight in this connection. This is because mortality changes normally tend to affect all ages in the same direction. It can be shown that if death rates at all ages improve by, say, a uniform ten per cent, the age structure of the population will not be affected.[12] Normally when there is an improvement in child mortality, for example, adult life is also healthier, and it is only by a differentially greater improvement (or deterioration) in mortality at one age than at others that the age structure of the population is affected. If, as in nineteenth-century Europe, the improvement in health causes a much bigger fall in child and adolescent mortality than in mortality later in life the effect is to increase the proportion of the population in the younger age-groups; the age pyramid thickens at the base. If, on the other hand, almost all lives which can be saved in early life are already preserved by modern public health and medical measures, as in advanced countries today, then any further saving in life must be among the middle-aged and elderly. This will thicken the pyramid towards its apex.

Contrary to the impression which still prevails at times, the increasing proportion of old people in the population of Europe is primarily due not to the great fall in mortality in the last century

Table 1·3 Age distribution in four model populations with different combinations of fertility and mortality [13]

Expectation of life at birth (in years)	GRR	Percentage of stable population		
		0–14	15–59	60 plus
30	3·0	41·3	54·5	4·1
70·2	3·0	47·3	48·4	4·3
30	1·5	24·7	63·8	11·5
70·2	1·5	29·3	57·7	13·0

and a half, but to the fall in fertility which has occurred. If there had been no change in fertility in European countries since 1800 while mortality had followed its historic path the proportion of the population in the younger age-groups would now be larger than it then was, and the proportion in the older age-groups no greater. This is the type of age structure which will become established in the developing countries in the next few decades if their present high fertility and new low mortality continue long enough for a stable age structure to emerge (see table 1·3, lines 1 and 2).

In fact, of course, European fertility has fallen heavily in the last hundred years, in most countries by a half or more. This change in the absence of mortality changes would have caused a rapid ageing of the population from the base of the pyramid; a marked relative widening in the upper steps of the age pyramid. The mortality changes, however, have worked in the opposite direction during most of the period, the fall in infant and child mortality tending to offset the fall in the birth rate, so although populations have aged, they have aged less than the fertility changes alone would lead one to expect (or more precisely the proportion in the younger age-groups has fallen considerably less than would otherwise have been the case, though the proportion in the upper age-groups has risen slightly more). The first and last lines of table 1·3 show what might be termed typical pre-industrial and post-industrial situations, and in addition the cross combinations of their characteristic fertility and mortality. If fertility had fallen without any change in mortality from a GRR of 3·0 to 1·5 the percentages in the three broad age divisions would have been 24·7, 63·8 and 11·5. In fact a great improvement in death rates occurred and this mitigated the violence of the change in age structure. In particular the proportion of children under 15 fell notably less. This is clear from the last line of the table where the three percentage figures are 29·3, 57·7 and 13·0.

Population and society

The statistics of population behaviour in the mass are a dry topic treated in isolation, though they possess their own fascination and rational structure. But they measure events which are central to the life of men and women in all ages. Once attention is turned outwards from the events themselves to the social and economic environment in which they occur, the appeal and importance of demography is apparent. The pressures of hard times and the opportunities of happier periods are reflected in historical demography like images in a camera obscura. The picture always needs interpretation and may lack the polychrome fullness of historical reality but it forms a clear and dependable outline to which colour may be added as the population characteristics are related to their social and economic setting.

It is easier to demonstrate the existence of close links between population, economy and society in history than to do justice to their analysis, for the relationships are very intricate. Some of the difficulties will grow clearer in later chapters. One may perhaps be mentioned now. It is that some terms are common to each branch of investigation but are used in slightly different senses. The word family, for example, has no single and precise meaning. It is sometimes used to mean all those living in a single household including servants, and in earlier times apprentices, as well as those related by blood or marriage to one another. Sometimes it is used to refer to a large group of relatives whether they all live under the same roof or not; sometimes confined to the conjugal family of father, mother and children, either living together or without this restriction; sometimes even confined to the siblings (brothers and sisters) within a single conjugal family. Again it may be used to cover only the children alive at one time or extended to all offspring of a marriage whether living or dead, as when demographers talk of completed family size. Often the context may make the meaning clear, but it is obvious that conceptions may quickly lose precision where terms can carry so many meanings.

A great deal of work both empirical and theoretical remains to be done before historical demography reaches the point at which its potential interest and importance are matched by its performance. Even now, however, the fascinations of the study of populations in the past far outweigh the frustrations. Perhaps indeed the most fascinating time of all in the development of a subject comes when its possibilities have grown plain but only a fraction of the source material has been sifted and the techniques and unifying concepts are still at the stage of rapid change and improvement.

2 The size of populations

2 The size of populations

The mechanisms discussed in chapter 1 may help to make clear how a balance may be reached between births and deaths. They bear, however, only on the ways in which a given size of population may be maintained, and not upon the question of the level at which this equilibrium occurs. Some initial light may be thrown on this subject by considering a few simple models. In later chapters some of the complexities of historical reality will be explored more fully.

The most influential discussion of this question ever published came from the pen of Thomas Malthus. The *First essay on population* was published in 1798 during the period which in retrospect we describe as the industrial revolution. But Malthus was a child of traditional Europe, of the period before the industrial revolution, and like his contemporaries he saw the land as the ultimate source of all material wealth. Twenty years earlier Adam Smith had written a passage in the *Wealth of Nations* which epitomises this admirably. Discussing the exchange of products manufactured in towns for the food and industrial raw materials produced in the countryside, he wrote:

It is this commerce which supplies the inhabitants of the town both with the materials of their work and the means of their subsistence. The quantity of the finished work which they sell to the inhabitants of the country necessarily regulates the quantity of the materials and provisions which they buy. Neither their employment nor subsistence, therefore, can augment, but in proportion to the augmentation of the demand from the country for finished work; and this demand can augment only in proportion to the extension of improvement and cultivation. Had human institutions, therefore, never disturbed the natural course of things, the progressive wealth and increase of the towns, would, in every political society, be consequential, and in proportion to the improvement and cultivation of the territory or country.[1]

Adam Smith here stated in a general form the basic thesis on which Malthus case rested – that the productivity of the land is the hinge of all economic life – though Malthus expressed this idea in a more restricted form, asserting that the maximum flow of food which can be squeezed from the land at any given level of agricultural technique sets an upper limit to the size any population can reach.

As long as population was well below the ceiling set in this way, Malthus supposed that population would grow rapidly, and at a constant rate. He claimed that the 'passion between the sexes' was a very potent driving force which ensured rapid and constant increase of population in the absence of any serious obstacle to growth. And to illustrate this point he frequently referred to the rate of increase of population in the North America of his day, where he believed the population to be doubling every quarter century. Yet however large and rich the country and however small the population at any given moment, simple geometrical progression ensured that the gap between present population and the maximum which could be supported would close rapidly. As population neared the ceiling both positive and preventive checks appeared to slow the increase and eventually to bring it to a halt.

Positive checks are those which increase mortality: preventive checks are those which lower fertility (Malthus thought mainly here of a later age of marriage). The former will normally affect most severely those whose circumstances of life are least easy. Amongst them as population rises disease and malnutrition will take an increasing toll. The interplay of fertility and mortality in terms of which Malthus conducted his argument may be illustrated graphically. Figure 2·1 shows what might be called the medium possibility. Fertility and mortality do not vary while population is anywhere below A in total numbers. Thereafter, however, both positive and preventive checks appear as the pressure upon food supplies, or more generally upon the resource base of the community, grows greater. Eventually the two schedules intersect at B, and population ceases to grow. As Malthus clearly understood, however, other points of intersection are equally possible according to the assumptions made about the onset of positive and preventive checks as pressure on the land increases. Figure 2·2, for example, shows the schedules of fertility and mortality in a situation in which preventive checks operate only slightly and very late in the day, though positive checks conform to the same pattern as in the previous figure. The population will rise to a substantially higher total than in

Figure 2·1 An illustration of the way in which fertility and mortality levels might change as population density increases to produce a stationary population at **B** (medium fertility hypothesis).
Figure 2·2 An illustration of the way in which fertility and mortality levels might change as population density increases to produce a stationary population at **D** (high fertility hypothesis).

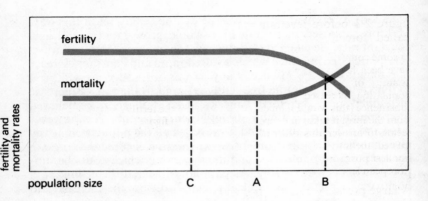

'Forced' High Death Rates, Medium Fertility - Misery

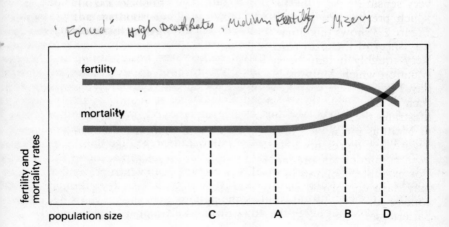

figure 2·1 before levelling off. This is a situation which Malthus called 'forced'.

In some countries population appears to have been forced; that is, the people have been habituated by degrees to live almost upon the smallest possible quantity of food. There must have been periods in such countries when population increased permanently, without an increase in the means of subsistence [this would happen, for example, if the fertility schedule changed from the form it takes in figure 2·1 to the form in figure 2·2 – my note]. China seems to answer this description. If the accounts we have of it are to be trusted, the lower classes of people are in the habit of living almost upon the smallest possible quantity of food, and are glad to get any putrid offals that European labourers would rather starve than eat.[2]

A large proportion of the population in these circumstances is very close to the Malthusian precipice and may be pushed over it in large numbers by even a moderately poor harvest. There is almost no cushion against disaster such as is to be found, say, at C on either figure, the position of the fortunate Americans.

Equally, it is possible to imagine a population in which the mortality schedule is still the same, but the fertility schedule reacts very sensitively to rising numbers (or in Malthusian language, in which preventive checks are evident early and are widespread). Figure 2·3 shows this situation. Here the total population falls some way short of the sizes reached in either of the two earlier figures. Very roughly it may be said that figure 2·1 corresponds to the situation which Malthus believed to exist in England in his own day. Figure 2·2 shows the extremities of misery reached in countries such as China or India. Position C on each of these two figures illustrates the happy position to be found in North America where, as Malthus put it, 'the reward of labour is at present so liberal'.[3] Figure 2·3 represents a type of situation which may well have been commoner in pre-industrial times than is usually supposed. For example, Colyton in Devon in the later seventeenth century may have conformed to this model at least as far as fertility is concerned. And many more primitive peoples followed this pattern (see pages 86–9).

Figure 2·4 shows the connection between the total size of population and standards of living or real incomes per head in Malthus' world. There will be a total population size so small that living standards suffer. This might be true, for example, if numbers were too small to permit the division of labour to be pushed as far as the technology of the day would otherwise permit; or if the population were too small to generate enough traffic to justify the creation of an adequate road network. Equally in terms of Malthus' model there must be a level of total population beyond which further increase inevitably depresses living standards. It follows from this that there must also be an optimum size of population. It may well take the form of an almost flat plateau rather than a sharp peak when represented graphically, but its existence is a corollary of this scheme. In figure 2·4 the combinations of fertility and mortality shown in the previous figures are represented by the points **A** to **E**. It is easy to see how much worse off the Chinese peasants are (**D**) than, say, the settlers in North America (**C**), and how this is connected with the pressure of population on the agricultural resource base.

The term optimum population is convenient to use in this context, but the simple term conceals the complexity of any concrete historical situation. A population level which approached the optimum from the point of view of a peasant or labourer, whose earning power rises if land is abundant and labour in short supply, may be far below the optimum seen through the eyes of a land-owner whose returns in this situation will be much less than would be the case with a larger labour supply and more men anxious to gain a footing on the land as tenants. And the size of population which may appear optimal if the analysis is conducted in terms of military power may be quite different from the level defined simply in economic terms. Accordingly it is justifiable to use the term without qualification only in order to get the discussion off the ground, as it were. In a fuller analysis much of the interest would stem from the refining of this rather woolly general concept.

The three sets of fertility and mortality schedules which have been examined represent, of course, only a few among the many possible combinations. It is possible, for example, to keep the fertility schedule constant and alter the mortality schedule to produce the same population totals as those just discussed. And if both types of schedules are altered a further range of possibilities is opened up. The general characteristics of models of this sort are plain, and do not require further elaboration. But how far does a range of models like these help in understanding the totals of population reached in the course of history?

The answer to this question depends very largely upon the type of society and economy in question. Least difficulty is occasioned by those whose material culture was most primitive. Groups which were dependent for their livelihood upon hunting, fishing and gathering were faced by a problem still simpler and starker than that which Malthus contemplated. In these societies there could normally be no question even of arithmetic addition to the supplies of food available. Food supplies might and did fluctuate widely from one season to the next and from year to year, but there could no more be any permanent gain in the size of the food base for such peoples than for animal species. At long intervals an exception to this rule might occur when an advance in material culture made a new source of food available (for example by the devising of a bow powerful enough to bring down a large animal which could not previously be killed), but for convenience of exposition it may be ignored.

Information about levels of fertility and mortality obtaining in these societies and about the social control of numbers is very limited and often imprecise, but it seems likely that their patterns of behaviour in this respect bore a strong resemblance to those which can be observed in many animals. A brief description of the relationship between animal social conventions and the regulation of animal population numbers, therefore, is a convenient point of departure for the study of primitive man.

Figure 2·3 An illustration of the way in which fertility and mortality levels might change as population density increases to produce a stationary population at **E** (low fertility hypothesis).

Figure 2·4 The relationship between population density and living standards on Malthusian assumptions.

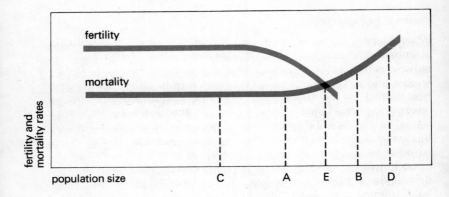

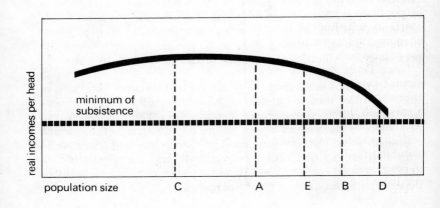

Animal populations

When Darwin wrote '. . . we have every reason to believe from what is known of wild animals that *all* would pair in the spring', but, conscious both of the vast powers of multiplication possessed by all species and of the absence of any long-term upward trend in numbers, added 'In the majority of cases it is most difficult to imagine where the check falls . . .',[4] he began a discussion which has continued to this day. The argument in Darwin's time and even today has many common elements with Malthus' scheme, as is, of course, to be expected in view of the influence which Malthus exercised upon him. The relentless press of new life provided Darwin with a driving force to energise his theory of natural selection. His rather bald statement in this passage implies a view of animal fertility which is not, to use the jargon, density-dependent. '. . . *on an average*', he wrote, 'the amount of food for each species must be constant; whereas the increase of all organisms tends to be geometrical, and in a vast majority of cases at an enormous ratio'.[5] And again, 'There is no exception to the rule that every organic being naturally increases at so high a rate, that, if not destroyed, the earth would soon be covered by the progeny of a single pair'.[6] There is no allowance here for any major fall in fertility as density of population increases. It implies a combination of fertility and mortality schedules of the type shown in figure 2·2 above. Fertility changes little as numbers rise but mortality gradually increases to the point where no further growth can take place.

Since Darwin's time, however, much observational and experimental evidence has shown that in very many cases fertility in animal populations is density-dependent just like mortality. Experiments with the water flea *Daphnia* show a steady decline in fertility with increased crowding. Many insects display a falling fertility with increasing population density, partly because of a shortage of suitable sites for the placing of eggs, and partly because of changes in behaviour brought on by overcrowding. The guppy, a fish which produces live offspring, multiplies freely until a certain density level has been reached and then eats up any further young within a few minutes of birth. This change in behaviour takes place while the adult guppy is adequately nourished and in good health. It is not of course strictly speaking a restriction of fertility, but like infanticide in human societies may be regarded as such.[7]

In these examples the decline in fertility as population rises appears to be a direct effect of increasing density of population upon individual activity. But there is a further range of methods developed by animal societies to keep population size within bounds which appears to have much in common with the behaviour of men and women in primitive societies. Selection in these animals has favoured the development of social conventions which help to regulate fertility. The general purpose served by these conventions seems to be to ensure that the numbers of a species in a given area do not rise to the point where adult members of the group find it difficult to keep in good health because of food shortage. To exceed a certain limit in this respect would prejudice the efficiency in the struggle to survive not only of the individuals immediately affected but also of the group as a whole. Wynne-Edwards states that with the rarest exceptions it is 'a matter of special remark . . . that the ceiling is never imposed by starvation'.[8] Selection will favour groups which are relatively few in number and are able for this reason to keep in good health. Any danger that excessive pressure on the supply of food might upset the local ecological balance and reduce the food base of the population is also averted in this way.

The social conventions developed either to reduce fertility well below the maximum theoretically attainable, or to induce a very high mortality among the very young take different forms in different species. In many bird species, for example, if numbers are rather large when the breeding season begins it may be impossible for some adults to secure a suitable territory in which to mate, nest and rear young. This happens with the great reed-warbler and probably with other territory nesting birds. Some sexually adult birds in these circumstances may pass the breeding season without mating (much as many Irish peasants' sons who did not succeed to land have had to choose between emigration and celibacy). In the case of other birds, like the white storks, adult members of the community who are low in the pecking-order not only may find it difficult to secure a nest site, but even if they find one, may rear very few viable offspring because of the pressures to which they are subjected by birds higher up the hierarchy. A socially-induced low fertility or high foetal or infant mortality, in short, may be observable: '*The function of the hierarchy, in fact, is always to identify the surplus individuals* whenever the population density requires to be thinned out . . .'.[9]

A wide range of further means exists in various species to secure similar effects, such as the prolonging of adolescence beyond its normal span. Even where the precise mechanism which secures a reduction of fertility is not fully understood, its effectiveness may often be observed. For instance, after outbreaks of myxamatosis had almost wiped out rabbit populations over large areas of England buzzards seldom bred except where rabbits had been little affected or where they had never been numerous.[10] There is evidence to suggest that in many animal species a large part of all social activities is connected with the sensitive and exact control of population size, though it must be added that the interpretation of much of this evidence about animal behaviour is still disputed. In all this the available supply of food remains the ultimate controlling factor but is not the proximate agent of control, at least for most species in stable environments.

The consideration of animal population behaviour is valuable because it suggests parallels between the social activities of men and animals in population control. If a woman in an Australian aboriginal tribe is burdened with more than one child which needs adult assistance to keep up with the group in its wanderings, not only will she be slowed down and her life and her children's lives be placed in danger, but the whole tribe may also suffer. This will happen either if the tribe abandons her and so loses the assistance of an important member, or if it is reduced in mobility because of her presence encumbered with children. In these circumstances it is not difficult to see why tribes which throw up a pattern of attitudes and behaviour which reduce the likelihood of such a situation occurring will be at a selective advantage as a group. This will be true, of course, whether or not the connection between the social convention and the end gained is recognised by the individuals who may be called upon to act.

There were a great variety of practices current among hunting, gathering and fishing tribes and others of primitive material culture which served to restrict fertility, often drastically. Long periods of suckling before weaning were almost universal. This reduces the chance of conception. In some cases during the suckling period, which might extend to two years or even more, there was also complete or partial abstention from intercourse. The Djuka of Dutch Guiana, for example, were strict in this respect.[11] When intercourse did take place attempts were made in some communities to ensure that conception did not occur. *Coitus interruptus* was known and practised in many communities in Africa, and has been reported elsewhere, notably in Tikopia.[12] Anal coitus and other deviant forms of intercourse were not uncommon in some societies.[13] And the use of contraceptives has also sometimes been noted. Usually the methods employed were not very effective, but occasionally powerful spermicides were employed. The Achehnese used a tannic acid suppository which could provide a good measure of protection.[14] Again, abortion was widely practised in many primitive societies in the past.

Nor was the period of danger over if the mother went to term. At this time in some communities the mother was temporarily isolated from the rest of the tribe and forced to fend for herself and her baby. Among the Siberian Ghiliak women were exposed at childbirth even in the bitterest weather.[15] In addition infanticide claimed very many new lives. The Arunta in Australia did not hesitate to kill children if there was an older child in the family still in need of nourishment from the mother.[16] Among the Bangerang, Narrinyeri and Kurnai children were similarly killed to prevent the mother having to carry two children.[17] In Africa there were tribes in which the child was killed if born feet first; others in which all twins were killed; yet others in which a child who cut his upper teeth first was regarded as cursed and put to death.[18] Frequently a much higher proportion of girl than boy babies was killed. Among the Netsilik Eskimos 38 cases of female infanticide in 96 births were noted.[19] This is probably an exceptionally high proportion, but infanticide has been noted among tribes in many parts of the world often bearing more heavily on girls than boys. And killing girl babies is, of course, a more effective means of limiting fertility than killing boys. Even where young babies were not actually killed they might customarily be exposed to great physical ordeals which must often have resulted in early death, as among the Thlinkeet or Nootka who rolled their children in snow and bathed them in water at near-freezing temperatures.[20]

In some cases actions which served to limit the flow of new life into the community were undertaken without any conscious appreciation of their importance in limiting population growth. Breach-born children, or those unfortunate enough to cut their teeth in an unusual sequence were destroyed because of the ill luck thought to attend them. And injunctions against the early resumption of intercourse after the birth of a child were seldom if ever imposed because of a conscious understanding of their effect upon the rapidity of family formation. In other cases it is clear that either the individual family or the community was quite conscious of the importance of restricting fertility in order to make life more tolerable for the living. Among the Tikopia, for example, living on a small island, there was a very keen appreciation of the importance of keeping families small so that a community of moderate size could preserve its amenities and keep strife within limits.[21] The Rendille camel herders in Kenya, conscious that the size of their flocks must limit their own numbers, have attempted to meet their difficulties in several ways, including infanticide and customs which delay marriage for women.[22] An instance has even been quoted of a child in an Australian tribe being killed in order to enable the mother to continue to suckle a puppy.[23] If true, this represented a determination to maintain or improve nourishment of the existing community rather than to add to its number. In many such communities, with or without conscious recognition of the results of low fertility, there was strong social pressure to keep families small. This might take the form of inducing a strong feeling of shame if children followed one another too quickly, as among the Motu Motu of New Guinea who were ashamed if a second child arrived before its older brother or sister could walk, though without going to the lengths of killing the newcomer.[24] Or at the other extreme of formality, there might be a consultation among the elders of a tribe to decide the fate of a recently born child as with the Australian Wadthawing.[25]

The cumulative effect upon fertility of all these practices and attitudes is very difficult to quantify in the absence of reliable and complete statistics. But it seems fair to suggest that, as with many animal societies, these human societies demonstrate the advantage in group selection of a socially limited fertility which serves the interests of the group as a whole better than unrestricted fertility would do. Whatever the origin of practices which limited fertility, their continued survival suggests that at worst they proved no handicap and that in many cases, however brutal or unfeeling they may appear to modern eyes, they were advantageous in the circumstances of the day. They gave rise to a fertility schedule which caused population numbers to stabilise at a level low enough to permit adult members to be adequately fed – a situation which has obvious parallels with animal societies.

Agricultural economies

With the development of agriculture and the domestication of animals the discussion of the question of population totals becomes more complex. The immediate effect of the cultivation of plants for food purposes, sometimes called the Neolithic food revolution, was of course to raise the population ceiling to a very much greater height than in the hunting and gathering communities. Whereas a population density of the order of one person to every ten square miles (25 square kilometres) was perhaps somewhere near the middle of the range of densities met with in hunting and gathering economies (the extremes might vary from this by, say, a factor of ten), settled agriculture can well support 25 people to the square mile (here again the range of densities varied from this figure by a factor of ten, though occasionally extremely high figures are encountered, notably in the most fertile 'rice basins' of south and east Asia).[26] If the transition from one condition to the other had been abrupt populations could clearly have grown very quickly for a considerable period before once more experiencing the difficulties caused by pressure on the food-base of the society. But the transition was not abrupt, nor when it had occurred was the new ceiling rigid in the same sense that the old had been. It would be foolish even when considering the material culture of pre-agricultural groups to ignore altogether the possibility of technical advance broadening the effective food-base of the group, but for most groups supported by a hunting and gathering economy change was probably very slight for very long periods. For tens or even hundreds of thousands of years changes in material culture may have had less influence on the quantity and type of animal and vegetable food available than the climatic changes of the Ice Ages.

In agricultural societies, on the other hand, advance in technique is an ever-present possibility. Advances may be small and relatively unimportant, as for example with the invention of the horse-collar to allow the strength of the animal to be harnessed more effectively to a plough or cart. Or they may be the means of a revolutionary expansion of the food-base, as with the introduction of the potato in many areas. And there is a wide range of improvements lying in between the two extremes – improvements in breeds of cattle or sheep; the elimination of fallow by the introduction of clovers, vetches and root crops; the development of better means of storing grains and other foods; and so on.

The perpetual possibility that an advance in material culture may raise the productivity of the land significantly makes the analysis of

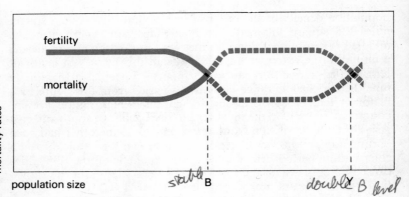

Figure 2·5 One possible result upon population size and schedules of fertility and mortality of an advance in material technology producing a doubling of food supplies.

fertility

mortality

fertility and mortality rates

population size   ~~stable~~ B   ~~double B level~~

population size a more complicated matter than is the case with hunting and gathering societies. The simplest case is illustrated in figure 2·5. This seems to have been the case which Malthus supposed normal. A population reaches a stable total at **B**, and re-remains at this level until a major advance in the material technology of the society doubles the supply of food and other agricultural raw materials which can be produced from the soil. When the new opportunities occur the checks both positive and preventive are relaxed, and fertility and mortality revert to the levels they displayed when population was building up towards the earlier total size. When the opportunities afforded by the advance in technology have been exhausted, however, the increase is slowed down and a new equilibrium total is reached at **Y** similar in all respects to the previous one except that the total size of the population has doubled. Living standards will again be what they were before, having briefly risen considerably during the period of lesser population pressure. The effect on living standards of the cycle of population growth may be seen in figure 2·4. During the period of rapid growth real incomes will rise quickly from **B** along the curve to **C**, but as the checks again appear the path along the curve to **B** will be retraced.

The relationship between advances in material culture and population growth, however, is much more complicated in most instances than this first analysis suggests; and this for three reasons. First, it is entirely possible that the combined schedules of fertility and mortality which kept population at its earlier level will not reappear when pressure upon the agricultural base again rises. Secondly, advances in material culture do not usually take place in discrete and decisive steps but irregularly and over a period which means that instead of the ceiling being raised with a violent jerk, it is edged up slowly and almost continuously. This must be true if only because new inventions spread slowly through any population at first and indeed several types of technology may co-exist for centuries or even millennia. In Sweden, for example, the plough took 3,000 years to oust the axe and fire as a means of preparing land for cultivation.[27] An appreciation of this point may well lie at the back of Malthus' view that agricultural production might grow at least arithmetically, though this would not of course fully offset the powers of growth possessed by populations. Thirdly, neither optimum nor (except in a rather meaningless physiological sense) minimum living standards remain the same if there are substantial changes in material culture, so that it is improbable for this reason also that a new position will arise similar in all respects to the old except for the absolute size of population. These complications may be examined briefly in turn.

Suppose by way of illustration that the change in material culture which has taken place has had the effect of doubling the amount of arable land at the disposal of what is by definition a society largely rooted in the soil. This might be the case if, for example, a method were developed of using heavy clay lands which had previously been too heavy to work, or if a new drainage technique made it possible to remove surplus water from large areas of low-lying ground. With plenty of new land available we may suppose that many preventive checks would disappear and fertility rise sharply as a result. Suppose, for example, that most sons had previously been obliged to wait before marrying until either their father's holding was transferred to them, or a marriageable woman was found who held land in her own right, and that the average age at first marriage were high as a result, and the proportion of men and women who remained single all their lives also high. With land plentiful and labour short these restrictions on marriage could well disappear without either the individual or the community suffering thereby. Indeed if the average size of holdings rose the standard of life would also rise and the society would for a time be placed in the happy position of enjoying both higher living standards and a greater freedom to marry young. Population in these circumstances would tend to rise rapidly, especially as in all probability mortality would also be low, but as the new land became more and more fully taken up, a different course of events from that described in figure 2·5 might well occur.

The first possibility is what might be termed an 'Irish' course of events. When any new set of social customs becomes established, it develops a momentum of its own, and may no longer change in changing circumstances. If for many generations young men have married in early manhood this custom may survive into a period when holdings are much harder to acquire. Then either the land holdings will become fragmented, or the landless paupers in the society will multiply. In a word the fertility schedule proves insensitive to pressure upon agricultural resources and population will reach high absolute figures at the cost of lowered living standards. This is the high-pressure solution to the problem of finding a new equilibrium level of population. Positive checks (high mortality) rather than preventive checks will play the greater part in establishing this level and living standards will be much nearer the minimum than the maximum attainable with the material technology of the day. On the other hand, events may well follow a very different path. If during the period of an abundant supply of new land the average size of holding rises and real incomes grow, men may prove jealous of their new prosperity and protect it by developing, consciously or not, a schedule of fertility which enables them to maintain their comparative affluence. This may happen, of course, even though fertility during an interim period of spreading settlement has been temporarily very high. Figure 2·6 illustrates these two further possibilities. If population reaches **Z** before ceasing to grow the bulk of the population will live in misery. A population which stabilises at **X**, on the other hand, will live much further from the precipice. The second, low-pressure, situation might be called the 'English' solution. It has been said that the expectations of most classes in England increased permanently in the century after the Restoration,[28] and there is evidence also that during this century fertility in England was rather low. Certainly, population increased very little in this period while living standards were rising.

The second point to bear in mind in considering alternatives to the simplest possible course of change shown in figure 2·5 is the way in which advances in material technology are diffused through an economy. This process is slow because the diffusion of a new technique is often measured in centuries rather than decades. And it is important to note that this slow change may often be underpinned by the population changes themselves. The relationship between demographic characteristics and economic change is highly complex. It is naive to treat the demography of a society as a result of its economic constitution – as a dependent variable which can be read off from the economic functioning of the society once that is known. On the contrary, the course of population change may often serve to stimulate changes in material technology which in turn raise the population ceiling. The subtle and dynamic interrelationship between the two may help to explain why in so many pre-industrial societies in Europe and elsewhere the agricultural base of the economy slowly broadened. It has even been argued that population pressure was a *sine qua non* of technical advance in agriculture in pre-industrial societies.[29] This view is difficult to support in its starkest form but is a useful corrective to the opposite view that population growth always waits upon an advance in technique.

There remains finally the third major modification of the simplest possible model of the effect of a change in material technology upon population size. Malthus used to argue that after any adventitious

Figure 2·6 Two further possible results of an advance in material technology upon fertility, mortality and total numbers, leading to new equilibrium populations at **X** (higher living standards) and **Z** (lower living standards).

Figure 2·7 A possible rising trend in living standards (**A** to **A'**) in a population in which material technology is developing.

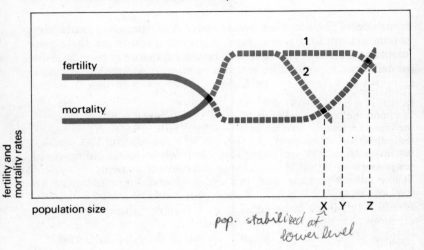

pop. stabilised at lower level

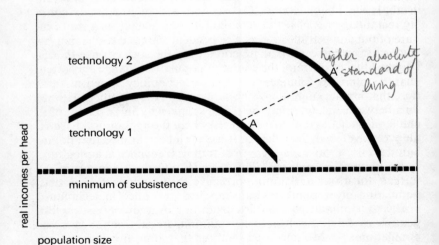

higher absolute standard of living

expansion of the food base of a society the inexorable pressure of population would sooner or later restore the previous ratio between people and resources, and that the chief mass of the people would be neither more nor less fortunately placed than earlier.

The happiness of a country does not depend, absolutely, upon its poverty, or its riches, upon its youth, or its age, upon its being thinly, or fully inhabited, but upon the rapidity with which it is increasing, upon the degree in which the yearly increase of food approaches to the yearly increase of an unrestricted population. This approximation is always the nearest in new colonies, where the knowledge and industry of an old State, operate on the fertile unappropriated land of a new one. In other cases, the youth or the age of a State is not in this respect of very great importance. It is probable that the food of Great Britain is divided in as great plenty to inhabitants, at the present period, as it was two thousand, three thousand, or four thousand years ago. And there is reason to believe that the poor and thinly inhabited tracts of the Scotch Highlands, are as much distressed by an overcharged population, as the rich and populous province of Flanders.[30]

Malthus' thesis may sometimes hold good, but it is not the whole truth. It is quite possible that after a period of widespread prosperity real incomes may be forced down to their old level by the pressure of population. Indeed figure 2·6 shows that their last state may in this respect be worse than their first if the fertility schedule proves less sensitive to pressure than in the past. But though it may be true that the minimum food needs of families do not change from age to age, that a man might live as miserably in the England of George III as in the England of William the Conqueror, it is also true that the living standards attainable by the most advantageous relationship between population size and production from the land rose substantially as advances in material culture took place. It would be ludicrous, for example, to suppose that the material culture of the Belgae, already an agricultural people using a heavy coulter plough, could possibly support a standard of life, even if the population size were optimal, as high as that attainable in England in the century of Adam Smith, Bakewell, Townsend, Coke, the Duke of Bridgewater, Telford, Newcomen, Watt, Boulton, Arkwright, Kay,

Darby and Cort. It is difficult to compare standards of life where material cultures are so different but it is hard to resist the conclusion that a man's productivity *might* grow substantially after advances had been made in material technology.

Figure 2·7 shows a possible result of successive improvements in material technology in an agricultural society. The maximum possible population is higher, and so is the maximum standard of living attainable, though the minimum remains unchanged. The highest and lowest points on the curves represent limiting cases, of course, which may never be reached by any particular historical society, but the general trend may well be upwards both for population totals and living standards, as long as advances in material culture are taking place. The dotted line A–A′ in figure 2·7 may possibly show the gross trend of events in pre-industrial Europe, with population A′ in the same relative position on curve 2 as population A on curve 1 but at a higher absolute standard of living. If this is true, it can only be so in the broadest perspective. In some countries over long periods matters fell out very differently. It may be that outside Europe, say in India, agricultural societies followed a different path because technological advances in the more recent centuries were less frequent and less important. It may well be also that a distinction should be drawn between what may be called intensive and extensive change in material technology. If a new technique increases the amount of cultivable land at the disposal of the community but without adding to the productive powers of individuals working on the land (extensive change) the effect on the living standards attainable at an optimum level of population will be less than if the change permits one man to produce more from the same area of land (intensive change).

The discussion of population size in this chapter has been very general and has not been anchored firmly in historical evidence apart from some scattered examples drawn mainly from hunting and gathering tribes. This has been a deliberate omission. There must always be some tension between clarity and comprehensiveness of exposition. But in recent years much more has come to be known about the characteristics of pre-industrial populations both in Europe before the nineteenth century and in some African and Asiatic areas today. The next chapter will include some of this empirical material. In it, moreover, some topics, notably the relationships between short and long term population fluctuations, which have been completely neglected in this chapter will be dealt with in some detail.

Before turning to these issues, however, we may take a first look at a topic which follows naturally from the preceding discussion – one of the cluster of subjects which fall under the general head of population and the industrial revolution. This is the title of chapter 5 and a general discussion of this question is to be found there. At this point, however, it is convenient to describe the sense in which the analysis of population size after the industrial revolution must be different from any treatment of the same point for pre-industrial populations; to emphasise the immensity of the difference between these two historical eras in demographic matters and particularly in the theoretical discussion of population size.

Industrial economies

It is ironical that Malthus should have written what he did when he did. However much details of his formulation of the problem posed by the inherent powers of increase of population may be criticised, his vision of a necessary tension between the press of population and the means of supporting it was just and is relevant to any study of conditions before his own day. And yet he was writing in the last years of its general relevance, for the industrial revolution brought in its train progressive changes in the productive powers of societies so great that the very concept of a ceiling has ceased to be useful for most purposes. The essential point is very simple. Once the productive power of society can be increased geometrically, and rates of economic growth of two, three and four per cent per annum or more can be maintained over long periods, a fact of demography which had previously seemed of only academic interest acquires suddenly a critical importance. For it is a fact that the reproductive powers of men and women are comparatively modest when compared with those, say, of the proverbial rabbit. Even on the most extreme assumptions no population is likely to be able to sustain a long term rate of natural increase as high as five per cent per annum. Four per cent has very rarely been attained and then only briefly; three is a rapid rate of growth; and, except in recent years in the developing countries, few populations have shown rates of growth as high as two per cent per annum. During the classic period of industrial revolution in Europe much lower rates still were normal. The largest single decadal increase of population in England and Wales, for instance, was 18·06 per cent in 1811–21, or a rate of 1·67 per cent per annum.[31]

Since populations can grow only rather slowly, while the production of wealth after an industrial revolution can expand quite quickly, it is always possible that the notional ceiling will recede above the rising population more quickly than the population itself can grow. Real incomes and standards of living can rise and did in fact rise in the nineteenth century. As they rose mortality fell but so, after a short time-lag, did fertility, and rates of growth in most western European countries remained modest (and in countries of new settlement like the United States or Australia where growth was much more rapid and populations might double in a quarter of a century, immigration provided a large part of the increase in population which occurred). With the powers of production possessed by society expanding geometrically in the way Malthus thought more typical of population, and population falling well short of the rates of growth theoretically attainable, the old tension so vividly depicted by Malthus no longer obtained. Moreover rates of growth of production have shown no clear signs of falling in industrial countries during the period since the industrial revolution and are unlikely to do so since the flow of important innovations shows no signs of slackening. Discussion of levels of maximum and optimum population have in consequence an air of unreality. Since it is perfectly possible both to achieve steadily rising real incomes

U.S. immigration policy ?

and to accommodate a fairly rapid rate of growth of population, analysis of population size in terms of a ceiling and a press of numbers beneath make no sense. Living standards measured by an economic yardstick have ceased to be a density-dependent phenomenon.

It may be objected to this very brief account of the implications of the industrial revolution for the analysis of population size that it fails to take account of the special importance of food supply. It is conceivable that industrial production might be able to expand very rapidly and without visible check and yet that because the supply of land is inelastic the difficulty of meeting the food requirements of the population might grow steadily. Malthus tended to cast his arguments in terms of the supply of food in particular rather than the production of goods and services of all types. It has been argued from time to time that only the opening up of large tracts of productive land in North and South America and in Australasia has enabled the countries of western Europe to escape Nemesis, and that their relief can only be temporary. Keynes himself used to argue that the long-term tendency of food prices must be to rise more than the price of manufactured goods because of the basic inelasticity of the supply of food since the acreage of cultivable land in the world as a whole cannot be increased indefinitely[32] (indeed it may tend to fall in the more densely populated countries such as Holland or England because of the constant drift of land into urban usage).

In order to gauge the force of this argument it is necessary to look more closely at the nature of the changes in the supply of raw materials of all sorts including food which took place during the industrial revolution. And this in turn is only possible if the situation in pre-industrial times is first described.

Although Malthus concentrated his attention mainly on the supply of food from the land his observations could be used with equal force in a discussion of raw material supply generally in pre-industrial economies (Adam Smith gave vigorous expression to the more general case in the passage quoted earlier in this chapter). Most forms of industrial production were as much dependent upon the productivity of the soil for their raw materials as was man for his food. The woollen industry could not continue without a supply of wool from the backs of sheep, nor the linen industry without flax. The industries processing and using leather needed a large animal population if they were to be able to sell their products at a price within the reach of potential buyers. The brewing industry kept land in barley and hops: and so on. More important than any other single industrial raw material was wood. Wood was necessary for the manufacture of almost all agricultural implements from ploughs to farm carts. It was the chief constructional material used in the transport industries both on sea and on land: ships and waggons were both made of wood. Even the earliest railways were made of wood, like those over which the horses dragged trucks from the pithead to the coal staithes along the Tyne. Wood was widely used in all types of industrial machinery, including many of the new machines of the industrial revolution itself. It was a major building material, entering into all types of construction, indeed it was almost the sole building material over large areas. Above all it was an essential raw material for the host of industrial processes – smelting, brewing, dyeing, salt-boiling – which depended upon a source of heat. Almost all the raw materials of industrial production in pre-industrial economies, in short, were either organic or, as in the case of mineral raw materials, could only be used if organic raw materials were available also.[33]

In these circumstances industrial production no less than the production of food clearly depends upon the productivity of the land. If, for example, as in thirteenth-century England, the pressure upon land becomes acute because of the rapid increase in population, and arable gains at the expense of pasture because more food per acre is produced in this way, then the number of cattle per head of population falls and the scarcity of leather increases. Or again, if the demand for wood for blast furnaces grows to the point at which the annual cut of timber exceeds the natural growth of the forests, as seems to have happened in the Weald of Kent and Sussex in the late sixteenth and early seventeenth centuries, then the industry must either contract *in situ* or move elsewhere. Simple calculations may be made which demonstrate how limited must be the volume of industrial output where the productivity of the land imposes a limit on the expansion of production. For example, it requires the growth of timber from 40,000 hectares (100,000 acres) of woodland to supply charcoal sufficient to make 10,000 tons of pig iron.[34] Even a level of iron production which today would be thought very modest would have denuded the forests of Europe in a few decades as long as wood was needed to turn the ore into metal. And one must not forget that wood was wanted also for naval spars, for beer barrels, for cart wheels, for furniture, for fencing, for a thousand and one other uses, which all increased the pressure on limited resources.

One essential aspect of the industrial revolution was the by-passing of the bottleneck caused by the problems of expanding organic raw material supply. The history of the substitution of coal for wood, first as a source of heat and later in the more complex chemical exchanges which take place in the smelting of metals, is long and intricate. All we need now note is that at various dates between the sixteenth century and the present day inorganic materials have come to be substituted for organic across a very broad spread of industrial products. These changes came early for some products; late for others. Coal was used instead of wood for boiling salt from seawater in salt pans in the sixteenth century. Nylon socks replaced woollen in the twentieth. Each such change removes another sector of industrial production from dependence upon the productivity of the soil.

It might seem that the shift from vegetable and animal raw materials to minerals is a case of 'out of the frying pan into the fire', since each ton of coal dug from the ground depletes irrevocably the store still to be exploited. There are many blighted areas, like the Borinage in Belgium or the west coast coalfields of Scotland, which bear witness to the difficulties which this may entail. But, though the cry of wasting assets has frequently been raised, the pace of technological change has always forestalled major crises.

The rapidly developing technology of generating electricity with power drawn from the heat of nuclear reactors is only one recent and dramatic example of this.

These changes in industrial supply are one important reason for the comparative ease with which the increased demand for food has been met. A far higher proportion of the total acreage in farm use can be devoted to the production of food for men, rather than the growth of food for draught animals or of industrial raw materials. Because tractors are now used on almost every farm, fodder once eaten by horses to provide energy to turn the sod, is now consumed by cows and eventually reaches the doorstep in milk bottles. Because coke is now used to smelt iron ore, great areas once kept as thick scrub to be cut over periodically for charcoal can be devoted to pasture. More important than these changes, however, has been the remarkable growth in the productivity of the land. An acre of wheat in England today yields about 30 cwts on an average (mean of the years 1959/60–1963/4).[35] An acre in the early eighteenth century yielded perhaps 11 cwts,[36] and even this figure was higher than in most of Europe at that time. In many industrial countries today governments are more concerned to keep the level of agricultural production low enough to maintain prices at a 'reasonable' level than to try to squeeze the last possible bushel from the soil to feed the hungry. The rotation of crops, the use of pesticides, the improvement of breeding stock, the selection of high-yielding plant strains, the liberal use of artificial fertilisers, irrigation, drainage, and the use of mechanically powered devices for all the main operations of the harvest year which frees the farmer from many of his traditional worries about getting the seed into the ground or the harvest reaped before the weather changes; all these have combined to produce a steady growth in productivity per acre. Meanwhile the productivity of agricultural workers has risen even more rapidly so that farms not only yield far more than in the past but can be worked by many fewer hands.

Even if an end to the rise in yields from the land were unavoidable it is doubtful whether society would have to face a constriction of population growth from sheer lack of food. Some types of food have already been synthesised directly from mineral elements on a small scale and this may well develop rapidly in the future. Indeed the synthesis of proteins on a commercial scale has already been suggested to help those countries in which diets are deficient in proteins. Food production, in short, like industrial production may become less and less dependent upon organic raw materials by the substitution of products made from inorganic raw materials. If this does happen it will justify Godwin in his refusal to give Malthus best on the question of increasing population, for he wrote in 1820:

. . . it is surely no great stretch of the faculty of anticipation, to say, that whatever man can decompose, man will be able to compound. The food that nourishes us is composed of certain elements; and wherever these elements can be found, human art will hereafter discover the power of reducing them into a state capable of affording corporeal sustenance. No good reason can be assigned, why that which produces animal nourishment, must have previously passed through a process of animal or vegetable life . . . . Thus it appears that, wherever earth, and water, and the other original chemical substances may be found, there human art may hereafter produce nourishment: and thus we are presented with a real infinite series of increase of the means of subsistence, to match Mr. Malthus's geometrical ratio for the multiplication of mankind.[37]

It does not, of course, follow from the foregoing that the rise of population in countries which have undergone an industrial revolution will not support an interesting analysis, only that a different set of considerations is more apposite. Nor does it follow that populations can increase indefinitely without serious problems arising. These two topics, however, can only be taken up when the nature of population history in the last two centuries in industrialised countries has been examined. Further discussion of these points is therefore best postponed to a later chapter.

3 Fluctuations in pre-industrial populations

3 Fluctuations in pre-industrial populations

In the last chapter we discussed population size in terms of the approach to a ceiling and the gradual strengthening of what Malthus called preventive and positive checks. This may be justified for pre-industrial populations, and as a way of exploring the relationships between a few important and general elements in the total population situation. But it fails of course to do justice to the complexity of population changes in the past. In particular we must take note of the fluctuations in population which occurred in pre-industrial societies, since they were often very drastic. Fortunately, for pre-industrial Europe there is now a large bank of information on which to draw.

Short-term fluctuations

In any closed population (that is one where there is no migratory flow either in or out) changes in numbers can occur only through birth and death. The process may be compared to the flow of water into a bath through a tap and its removal down a plughole. The capacity of the tap fixes the maximum possible inflow. Except where the age structure of the population is very unusual the maximum rate of inflow is about 50 per 1,000 per annum. Birth rates above this level are very exceptional and rates above 45 are uncommon. The volume of water in the bath, therefore, may be increased by a maximum of about a twentieth in any one year. At the other extreme the inflow might conceivably be nil (if there were no live births in the year in question), but this minimum could be approached only in a tiny population. In large pre-industrial populations minima would very rarely be less than 15 per 1,000.

In contrast to the comparatively narrow limits within which all variations in inflow must occur, the plughole in pre-industrial baths was very large in diameter. In bad years local populations sometimes experienced death-rates as high as 200, 300 and even 400 per 1,000. The volume of water in the bath could quite clearly be reduced very markedly in a very short period of time if seasons of this severity occurred. National, indeed continental, populations were also subject to appalling setbacks in really bad years. The Black Death reduced European populations over areas measured in hundreds of thousands of square miles by up to a third in a single year. And there were other periods when populations fell sharply over large tracts of Europe, for example during the famine years 1315–7. Disastrous mortalities continued to occur until early modern times. The population of Denmark fell by more than a fifth between 1650 and 1660.[1] One of the four counties of Finland, which was probably typical of the country as a whole, is estimated to have lost about 28 per cent of its population in the crisis years 1696–7.[2] Much of western Europe suffered heavy mortalities as recently as the series of bad harvest years between 1740 and 1743. In general, however, the larger the population the less extreme the peaks in mortality rates. Many seasons of high mortality were quite local in their incidence, caused by a local harvest failure, or by an outbreak of an epidemic disease affecting only a small area.

A sudden surge of mortality is *not* necessarily evidence of over-population. In many parts of Europe years of heavy mortality occurred periodically (roughly once every generation was a common pattern) even though population totals might be well short of the levels at which severe Malthusian checks were to be expected. The proportion of the population dying during bad seasons might be higher when numbers were approaching a maximum given the material culture of the day, but even where there was little or no population pressure of this sort there were still years in which very large numbers died. This was due in part to the independent importance of epidemic disease: some diseases, such as smallpox or influenza, might break out even though there was no threat of famine (though they would, of course, normally claim more victims in an ill-nourished population). But it was also due to the big swings in harvest yield which pre-industrial populations were obliged to accept as part of the order of things. Often the average size of the harvest over a period of a decade or so was quite sufficient to meet the needs of a local population, and yet two or three bad years might reduce food supplies to the danger level. The

*no way to send
local surplus elsewhere*

price of food would then shoot up and those whose reserves of cash were small died in large numbers. It was a common pattern in these circumstances for other members of a family to die in quick succession if the breadwinner died. The carryover of grain from one year to the next might enable a community to cope with the problem of a single bad harvest but was seldom adequate to meet the demands of two bad years in succession. Nor in general was land transport sufficiently cheap and flexible for local surpluses built up in other more fortunate areas to be moved easily to deficit areas. And effective demand might also be very slight if many families had exhausted their reserves of cash during a bad season in the previous year.

In all pre-industrial communities, too, whatever their general fertility and mortality schedules, social and political events might have a marked effect on mortality. Provident governments which took care to buy in and store grain in years of surplus could do much to mitigate the effects of harvest failure. Prolonged warfare on the other hand, though it might kill comparatively few men by the sword, might decimate population nonetheless. Armies harboured many diseases, notably typhus and venereal diseases, and as they moved about could spread them through wide tracts of country. In addition war took men off the land and in doing so reduced the production of food much as a bad harvest might. And war meant heavy taxes which took money away from those most in need of it to tide them over a poor harvest. Thus a moderately bad harvest sometimes produced an effect similar to a harvest failure. A man may faint from hunger even when food is not absolutely in very short supply if he lacks the means to buy what he needs. Dr Johnson was told that more than twenty people died weekly in London from the indirect effects of starvation.[3]

Goubert's classic study of the Beauvaisis is a rich mine of information about the short term fluctuations in local populations in pre-industrial Europe. Table 3·1 shows the extent of the fluctuations which occurred in the quarterly totals of conceptions, burials and marriages in the parishes of Auneuil, Breteuil and Mouy.

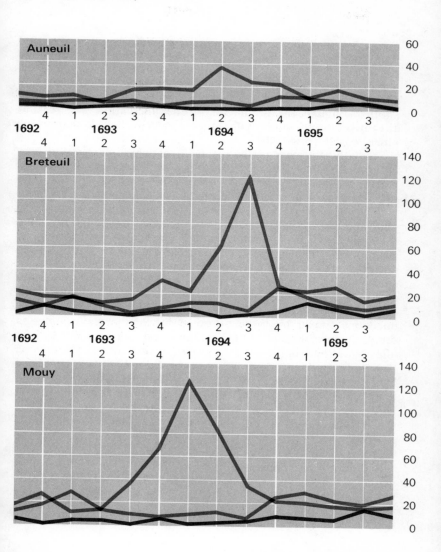

Figure 3·1 Changes in the number of conceptions, burials and marriages during a late seventeenth century demographic crisis in three French parishes (quarterly totals).

conceptions
burials
marriages

Figure 3·1 gives the same information graphically, while table 3·2 shows the course of wheat prices during this period. Several points call for comment.

First, the number of burials on the one hand and of marriages and conceptions on the other tend to move inversely to one another, though the amplitude of the fluctuation, for reasons already discussed, is normally much greater in burials than in the other two categories.

Secondly, the changes in the price of wheat correspond very closely with the changes in the number of conceptions, burials and marriages. Indeed Goubert has gone so far as to remark that 'The price of wheat almost always constitutes a true demographic barometer. The range and frequency of the fluctuations in grain prices control the size and the frequency of the demographic crises. And these play a large part in determining population movements and even its size.'[4] When the price of wheat was high the numbers of deaths increased sharply while the number of both marriages and conceptions fell abruptly. The deaths which occurred were seldom due to outright starvation but rather to diseases brought on or aggravated by eating rotten, ill-balanced and insufficient food, or to infections spread by those uprooted by famine and wandering desolate across the face of the land. Desperate starving men will eat offal, grass and bark; even on occasion each other. During the terrible Norwegian famine years in the early 1740s the people of Hallingdal were reduced to washing the dung from the straw in old dunghills to bake a pathetic substitute for bread.[5] A long respite between crises often meant that when the next one came its impact was the more severe. Goubert goes so far as to say that it is almost an absolute rule that the further away the last crisis, the worse the next proves to be.[6]

A third point to note about the crisis of 1693–4 in the Beauvaisis is that although it is apparent in all three parishes its impact was not uniform. It was much less severely felt in Auneuil than in either Breteuil or Mouy. The explanation lies in the economic constitution of the three parishes. Auneuil, the parish least affected, lies in

Table 3·1 The anatomy of a demographic crisis.[7]

Auneuil

Quarters	1692		1693				1694				1695			
	3	4	1	2	3	4	1	2	3	4	1	2	3	4
Conceptions	13	10	12	6	7	3	6	7	4	12	11	18	10	9
Burials	6	5	6	7	17	17	16	36	23	22	10	9	5	2
Marriages	3	3	0	1	2	1	0	0	0	1	1	4	5	2

Breteuil

Quarters	1692		1693				1694				1695			
	3	4	1	2	3	4	1	2	3	4	1	2	3	4
Conceptions	14	9	18	10	4	8	12	12	5	24	22	26	14	19
Burials	21	16	16	11	15	31	22	60	120	27	18	11	8	12
Marriages	3	9	4	3	1	4	5	0	2	4	12	7	3	7

Mouy

Quarters	1692		1693				1694				1695			
	3	4	1	2	3	4	1	2	3	4	1	2	3	4
Conceptions	18	28	12	13	10	8	9	12	7	25	29	22	19	26
Burials	12	18	29	14	37	67	124	82	35	21	20	17	15	17
Marriages	5	1	4	4	0	5	1	2	3	8	6	5	14	8

Table 3·2 Wheat prices
(in *sols* per *mine aux blés*)[8]

Year (harvest years beginning October)	Price	Year (harvest years beginning October)	Price
1690–1	35	1693–4	150
1691–2	54	1694–5	57
1692–3	95	1695–6	34

the south of the Beauvaisis in the *pays de Bray*. This was an area of mixed agriculture with an important pastoral element in the total rural economy. Here there were large areas of woodland and meadow. The more diversified the agricultural base of a community, the less likely it is to be crippled in years of distress and harvest failure. The same summer of constant rain which brings ruin to the wheat fields may yield a rich growth of grass and a larger production of meat and dairy products than usual. In the north of the Beauvaisis, on the other hand, on the high plains of Picardy where Breteuil is situated, a system had developed which might almost be called cereal monoculture. Here there were few beasts and very little of the countryside was uncultivated. Population was dense. The 'cushion' against harvest failure was slight and the results were devastating. Whereas the burial surplus in 1693–4 in Auneuil was about 12 per cent of the total population, in Breteuil it was about twice as great, and population recovered its previous level much less quickly.

In pre-industrial economies workers dependent upon rural industry were often even more exposed to fatal misfortune than those working on the land. The appalling mortality in Mouy is evidence of this. In this parish there was a large local woollen industry. In years of high corn prices (other grain prices moved in the same direction as wheat prices, though the cheaper grains displayed even more violent fluctuations than wheat because demand shifted towards the lowest-priced grain when supplies generally were short) not only were those who depended chiefly upon money payments sure to feel the pinch hardest, but cloth workers were still more hard-hit than most because the whole weight of demand lurched out of the industrial into the agricultural sector in times of high food prices. This left textile workers out of employment just at the time when their need for money was at its most desperate.

A year of demographic crisis had the effect of weeding out many of those who were most vulnerable in a population, both in the economic and the physiological sense. Years of crisis were, therefore,

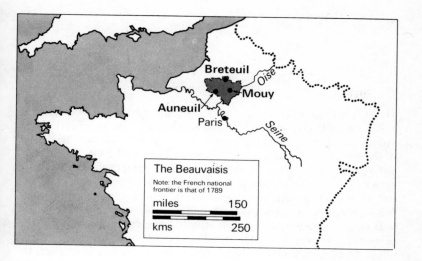

The Beauvaisis

Note: the French national frontier is that of 1789

miles 150
kms 250

normally followed by a period of much lower mortality. If there were untenanted holdings or unworked looms made available by death during the crisis, or if marriages had been postponed because of the hard times, a rush of new marriages followed and a spurt of births would coincide with the reduction in the numbers of deaths to give a few years in which population could rise rapidly. The rise in the number of births meant of course that twenty years after the crisis there was a sudden jump in the number of young adults, and if they were able to marry and begin families, this tended to set up a wave-like surge in numbers with a periodicity of about a generation. Each baby-boom produced an echo after the elapse of roughly a quarter of a century as the babies in question themselves began to form families. Eventually the pattern dies out if there are no further perturbations. Very frequently a further crisis blots out the pattern, but occasionally it is visible over a long period. This was remarked by the Norwegian sociologist Sundt and is sometimes known as Sundt's law. Table 3·3 shows how an earlier period of crisis in Norway which produced an irregular age distribution caused big discrepancies in the relative rates of increase of various age-groups in the nineteenth century. After 1809 no further large crises occurred and the effects of the troubled period were not obscured by similar, later disruptions. The interdependence of the movements in the different age-groups shows up clearly. The age-groups 20–9 and 30–9 grew very little in combined total between 1825 and 1835 (−1·8 per cent and 6·6 per cent respectively). These are the child bearing age-groups which explains the very slight rise in the number of children 0–9 between 1835 and 1845. In the next ten-year period (1845–55) the number of young children increased very rapidly – a reflection of the big increase in the age-group 20–9 over the period 1835–45, these young parents being the 'baby-boom' generation of the years 1815–25.

It is not surprising that crises should have recurred at an interval of about a generation since numbers could build up quite rapidly in such a period, even though minor crises, sufficient to convert the surplus of baptisms into a deficit, occurred much more frequently. For example, if between major crises the difference between the crude birth and death rates were ten per thousand per annum on an average (which was not an extreme figure for natural increase in such periods), this would mean an increase of a quarter in 23 years. After such an increase a population might be said to be ripe for a further severe check. Certainly this cycle of events is visible in the Beauvaisis in the later seventeenth and early eighteenth century when the secular trend of population was broadly horizontal. But the phenomenon was more general and is often found in pre-industrial populations even when the secular tendency was strongly upwards. An erratic and sometimes violent fluctuation round the trend line was characteristic of pre-industrial populations generally: it is not peculiar to a stationary, a rising, or a falling population.

But if the model of short term fluctuations in populations just described is typical of many parts of western Europe before 1800, it is far too simple to accommodate the full variety of patterns of population movement which may be observed. It is important, therefore, to amplify and modify the foregoing.

In the first place demographic crises were not to be found in all areas and periods. For example during the three centuries from 1558 to 1837 the mean number of baptisms in the parish of Hartland in Devon was 36; the mean number of burials 27. In only four of the 280 years was the number of baptisms 55 or more; in only

Table 3·3 An example of Sundt's law[9]
(percentage change in age-group sizes)

Age-group	1801—25	1825—35	1835—45	1845—55	1855—65
0—9	23·5	10·7	3·2	20·4	16·7
10—19	8·6	39·7	10·6	2·3	23·2
20—9	28·1	−1·8	38·8	8·5	−1·1
30—9	27·0	6·6	−0·3	31·5	10·1
40—9	2·2	22·6	5·3	−2·5	39·8

four less than 20 (the largest and smallest figures were 65 and 13). In only nine years were there 45 or more burials; in only 12 less than 15 (here the extreme figures were 69 and 8). Figure 3·2 shows the annual totals of baptisms and burials in the parish. The most striking feature of Hartland's population history when compared with that of a typical parish in the Beauvaisis is the rarity of any changes in the number of baptisms and burials which could not be the product of chance given the small number of events which took place each year.

Hartland is a remote parish in the north-west of Devon, square in shape and surrounded on two sides by the sea. It was almost entirely agricultural in economic activity. The agriculture was well diversified, which must have helped the inhabitants of Hartland to escape the distressing succession of crises which plagued the villagers of the northern Beauvaisis in the seventeenth century. And Hartland's remoteness from the chief highways of the kingdom no doubt helped to preserve the parish from plague and other epidemic diseases during this very long period. Nevertheless the contrast between the comparative tranquility of Hartland's population story and the periodic disruptions of the classic type of demographic

72

Figure 3·2
Baptisms, burials and marriages in Hartland 1558–1837.

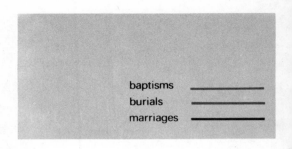

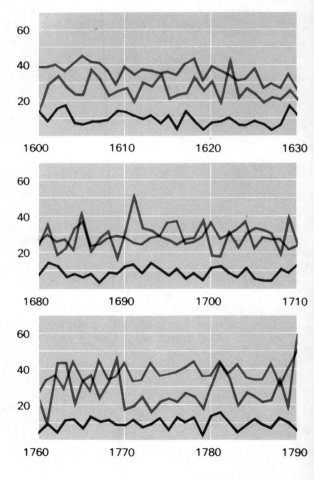

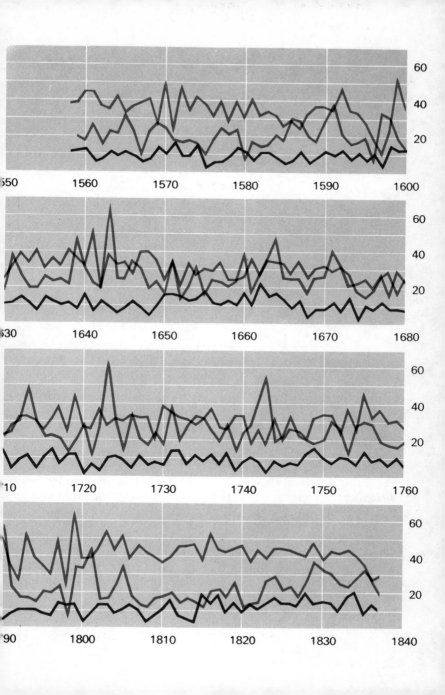

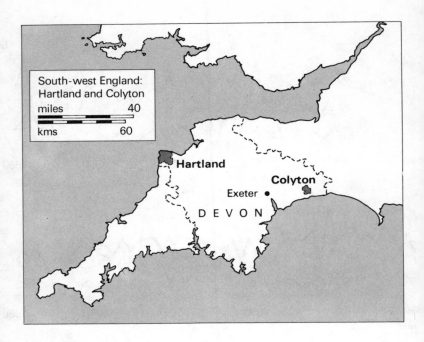

South-west England:
Hartland and Colyton
miles   40
kms   60

Hartland

Colyton

Exeter

DEVON

crisis is surely no freak. There are hundreds of English parishes whose history is closer to Hartland's than to that of Breteuil. Probably standards of living were higher in England than on the continent, and this, if it was so, meant a better cushion against years of poor harvest than in other countries. But even so, a diversity of experience must be expected in all countries. There were parts of France in which crises were rare and mild. Economy and society were local or regional rather than national, and population history followed suit.

Secondly, it would be unwise to lose sight of the importance of the heavy toll which might arise from epidemics pure and simple. Where these occurred there might be no tremor in the wheat price barometer to give warning of the deaths to come. In England the years 1557–9 were very sickly throughout the country with high mortality from a sweating sickness (which may have been a very severe type of influenza), though the price of provisions was not high in these years. The Exeter wheat price series gives no figure for

Table 3·4 Wheat prices[10] and burial fluctuations
(prices in shillings per Winchester quarter)

	Price	Burials in 29 parishes		Price	Burials in 29 parishes
1555	24·77	358	1559	20·64	704
1556	32·41	427	1560	22·62	409
1557	11·47	646	1561	15·50	336
1558	—	750			

The parishes are Colyton (Devon); Ardleigh and Stanford Rivers (Essex); Headley (Hampshire); Lugwardine (Hereford); Hunsdon and Berkhampstead (Herts); Wye, Biddenden, Tonbridge and Gravesend (Kent); Whittington (Lancs); Shepshed, Saddington and Melton Mowbray (Leics); North Elmham, Wells, Norwich St. Peter Mancroft and Norwich St Peter Permountergate (Norfolk); Saxmundham, Stradbroke and Wortham (Suffolk); Ellastone (Staffs); Frant (Sussex); Coleshill (Warwick); King's Norton (Worcs); Ledsham, Brodsworth and Kippax (Yorks).

the year 1558 but the years on either side run as in table 3·4, which also shows the number of burials in 29 English parishes scattered through 15 counties. If wheat prices were a barometer of mortality there would be every reason to expect the years 1557–9 to have been very healthy rather than especially fatal. Instead average mortality over the three years was more than 80 per cent higher than the average of the four years 1555–6 and 1560–1. Assuming that the crude death rate was normally about 30 per thousand, this means that it averaged 55 per thousand in 1557–9. Over this period it is safe to assume that the total population of the country fell by five per cent and possibly by a larger fraction, given that the 29 parishes are representative of the whole country. The mortality was notably widespread and is clearly evident in 22 of the 29 parishes. In only three was there no sign of unusual mortality in these years. In four a rise in the number of burials is visible but not large enough to suggest strongly a period of unusual ill health.

In pre-industrial Sweden, too, epidemic disease often wrought havoc without close relation to the harvest. The general pattern of mortality showed a complex relationship to economic and social life. Mortality was as a rule higher in the east, where harvest failure was uncommon, than in either the west or north which were much afflicted by poor harvests. Eastern Sweden had more large towns, different social conditions and tenurial arrangements, and a greater density of settlement, all of which may have helped to outweigh any direct effect of harvest and local food supply. Even in western Sweden the heavy mortalities of years in which the harvest failed were sometimes greatly aggravated by the apparently fortuitous incidence of epidemic disease as with the typhus of 1741.[11]

Finally, it is worth stressing again that men in pre-industrial economies were very much at the mercy of the elements. One farmer's meat might be another's poison. A year of light spring and summer rainfall with long warm spells might bring a bumper harvest to wheat growers on clay lands where the normal problem was disposing of surplus water, while bringing very thin crops to those farming the chalks and sands which were easily affected by drought. Weather was perennially important. All were vulnerable, but some were more vulnerable than others. Slight variations in summer temperature in, say, Beauce might make only a minor difference to the date of the harvest and its size. Similar variations in parts of Scandinavia might make the difference between a crop to be harvested and the failure of the grain to ripen at all. And the whole economy hinged on the harvest. Even in the early nineteenth century, and in England, it seemed natural to Thomas Tooke, when reviewing recent economic history, to regard the harvest as the most important single guide to the economic fortunes of the country from year to year.[12]

Long-term fluctuations

People who lived in pre-industrial Europe were vividly aware of the significance of the short-term population fluctuations which have just been described. Men lived their lives in a moving present and short-term prospects occupied most of their attention. Even the seven fat and seven lean years of scripture cover a longer span than would have entered into the calculations of most men. With the benefit of hindsight, however, long-term changes in the demographic characteristics of traditional societies are also visible.

If populations had conformed to the simple models described in the last chapter, it would be natural to expect that the secular trend of population would be upwards. Other things being equal each advance in material culture should have made possible a further inching up of numbers. In a very broad sweep of history it is true that the secular trend has been upwards, but the sweep must be very broad indeed if the trend is always to be found for, in addition to the frequent ups and downs which so often give a jagged, sawtooth appearance to a graph of annual totals of births, deaths and marriages, there were periods of centuries during which population totals were lower than before, or when population, though not declining, showed no upward trend. Long-term changes in population numbers in pre-industrial Europe produce a pattern rather like that of waves on a beach when the tide is coming in. Each wave may carry a little further up the sand than the last, but it is a result of both ebb and flow, not simply of a slow and steady advance across the beach.

In England after the Norman conquest and before the industrial revolution, for example, there appear to have been two full long-term cycles of population growth. During the period from the Conquest to the end of the thirteenth century the trend on this scale of analysis was upward (though if the time scale were the year, or even the decade, many periods of decline would be found even in these two centuries). This wave had spent its force by the beginning of the fourteenth century and ebbed back sharply when the Black Death took such a huge toll of life in 1348. There then followed a very interesting period lasting perhaps a century and a quarter during which population, though now much smaller in size than in the late thirteenth century, seems not to have shown any clear tendency to rise. In terms of models used in the last chapter

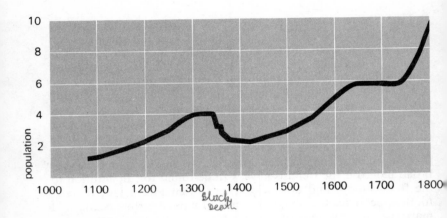

Figure 3·3 Long term population trends in England and Wales, 1000–1800 (in millions).

Black Death

this implies that either the fertility or mortality schedules or both changed considerably. Otherwise with much more land available per head of population and a higher standard of living for the mass of the population, numbers should have risen. At the end of the fifteenth century population again began to rise and by the time that the parish registers were first kept in 1538 population was rising fast in most parishes. It continued to do so until the middle decades of the seventeenth century, when this second wave of growth was played out and for a century population nationally showed no decisive trend. In some parts of the country, notably in the west, north and in Kent many registers yield totals of baptisms and burials which suggest that population was falling, though in the Midlands and Home Counties there may have been some further growth, and London grew rapidly. Finally, towards the middle of the eighteenth century there was a sudden fierce acceleration in population growth. Figure 3·3 shows the two cycles diagrammatically.

The causes of long-term fluctuations of this sort are obscure. Many different explanations have been advanced. It has been said, for example, that the population fall of the later Middle Ages was a result of climatic change with cooler and wetter summers replacing several centuries of more favourable climate. Quite small absolute changes in mean temperature can have important effects on the limits of cultivation. A fall in mean summer temperatures of one degree centigrade is equivalent to thrusting up the land surface about 500 feet about its former level, and takes many areas which were previously cultivable if marginal into the category of grazing land or rough pasture. In certain parts of northern Europe quite a substantial fraction of previously cultivable land might therefore pass into another category, with only a modest change in prevailing climatic conditions.

Alternatively, it has been claimed that the independent action of disease may explain the fall in population. Bubonic plague returned repeatedly to western Europe for a period of more than three centuries after the Black Death and it has sometimes been argued that this was sufficient both to cut back population drastically in the first terrible outbreak (when the plague occurred in its more deadly and much more infectious pneumonic form), and then periodically to prune down any incipient upwards movements for more than a century. At a later date smallpox has been accorded a similar, major independent role both in causing population growth to die away and, when inoculation and vaccination had become widespread, in permitting numbers to rise once more.[13] Virulent forms of dysentery, acting autonomously, may have caused population decline in parts of France and elsewhere in the last decades of the seventeenth century; and so on.[14]

The first of these two possible explanations is equivalent to a sudden lowering of the population ceiling, to use the terminology of the last chapter, while the second represents a substantial raising of the whole mortality schedule. Both could in principle produce a lower equilibrium level of total population for a time. Both rest upon slender foundations of empirical evidence, and even if this were greatly strengthened are rather *simpliste*. Complex situations are unlikely to be fully grasped by reference to a single cause. Each explanation may play some part in a full understanding of long-term fluctuations in population but in the present imperfect state of knowledge it is difficult to do more than list them as possible contributory causes. More strictly economic or sociological explanations have also been advanced but once more we lack the knowledge to subject logically consistent chains of argument to decisive empirical tests.

New demographic techniques

A basic problem here is that of knowing enough about the rates of flow of water into and out of the bath to be able to make good sense of the current water level. English population in the early fifteenth century was probably much the same size as in the mid-twelfth, but in the latter period numbers were still growing whereas in the former they were barely stationary. What was different about the demography of these two periods? Was it that the fifteenth-century fertility was lower? Or mortality higher? Or was there a combination of the two at work?

Until recently it seemed unlikely that conclusive answers to questions of this sort would ever be obtained for any period before the nineteenth century. For to measure fertility or mortality accurately a rate must be derived; and to derive a rate requires a knowledge both of the number of events in a class (say legitimate birth to mothers aged 25–9) and the population at risk (in this case the number of married women aged 25–9). For periods before the nineteenth century it was sometimes possible to obtain information either about the number of vital events or about the size of a population, but the two were very seldom both regularly available. And even when some data of both types were available they were often not very accurate and could not be broken down by age and sex in a way to permit the more precise measurements of fertility and mortality to be made.

Within the last fifteen years, however, a major breakthrough in the techniques at the disposal of historical demographers has taken place. This stands largely to the credit of Fleury and Henry whose development of the method of family reconstitution has made it possible to obtain a very full insight into the demography of any community which kept a full record of the vital events taking place within its boundaries.[15] The parish registers of several European countries (e.g. France, Italy and the Scandinavian countries) contain material of this type. Where family reconstitution can be employed successfully it provides measures of fertility comparable in detail and accuracy to those available for modern populations in developed countries. Mortality and nuptiality can also be studied in detail. In England a few parishes possess registers suitable for family reconstitution running from the mid-sixteenth century without a break. This makes it possible to trace in detail the demographic history of a community through the period of rapid growth in the sixteenth and early seventeenth centuries, and the stagnation or decline of the later seventeenth and early eighteenth centuries, to the renewed growth of the later eighteenth and early nineteenth centuries. It is of interest to describe briefly the history of one English parish in order to illustrate the range of demographic traits which may be observed in the course of a cycle of this sort. The provenance of these changes is not always clear as yet, but the extent of the changes is a matter of importance in itself since it shows how greatly the mortality and fertility schedules of pre-industrial communities might vary in the course of a few generations.

Colyton is a large parish of more than 7,000 acres near the mouth of the Axe valley in south-east Devon (see map on page 74). It consists of a small market town, Colyton itself; another smaller settlement, Colyford; and a scattering of small hamlets and isolated farmsteads. Agriculture in the parish was diversified, and as in so many other parts of England there was a local woollen industry, which formed part of the large cloth trade complex of Exeter, 20 miles to the west. The population of the parish was recorded as 1,641 when the first census was taken in 1801. During the three preceding centuries it fluctuated considerably, reaching a peak

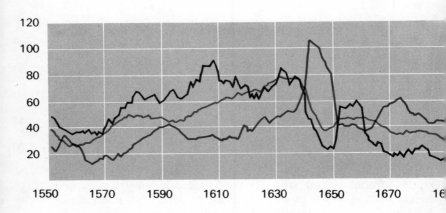

Figure 3·4 Baptisms, burials and marriages in Colyton[16] (nine-year moving averages).

probably slightly under 2,000 in the early 1640s but falling by about one third to a low point in the early eighteenth century. Figure 3·4 shows the fluctuations in baptisms, burials and marriages as nine-year moving averages. During the last century the record is not complete since some Nonconformist children were not baptised in the parish church and do not appear in the Anglican register. Deficiencies in the coverage of burials and marriages were probably much less, and the gross changes which took place are well enough shown by the graph. There was a great surge of population growth during the first century down to the 1640s. This came to a cataclysmic end when Colyton's last plague outbreak cut back population drastically (in the twelve months from the beginning of November 1645 to the end of October 1646, 392 names appear in the burial register, about a fifth of the whole population). For the rest of the seventeenth century and in the early decades of the eighteenth there was usually a surplus of burials over baptisms, and although this disappeared by the mid-1730s, a large surplus of baptisms was not again apparent until the 1780s.

The bare record of numbers of baptisms, burials and marriages

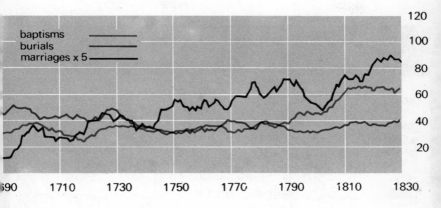

baptisms
burials
marriages x 5

is enough to suggest that great changes in fertility and mortality had taken place, but it is not sufficient to show what these changes were. Family reconstitution, by drawing together information about the members of many of the families which lived in Colyton during these three centuries, can go far to rectifying this. Figure 3·5 shows the range of information which can be recovered in favourable circumstances. William Hore's was one of those families fortunate enough to escape with no more than the quota of mortality early in life to which all men were accustomed in pre-industrial times. His wife Johane bore him children roughly every second year through two decades of their life together, and of their eleven children only two died in early infancy. Charyttye died in the prime of youth. The others either lived to a good age or had moved away from the parish which is proof that they had at least survived childhood. Eddythe lived and died a maid having outlasted all her brothers and sisters whose fate is known. It was entirely in accord with the usage of that time that the children's father William should have remarried so soon after the death of his first wife. Remarriages within a period of weeks rather than months were not uncommon.

Figure 3·5 William Hore's family
(an example of family reconstitution).

HUSBAND	HORE	surname	William	name(s)		Son	Harry Agnes CONNANTE John*		Occupation		husband shoomaker
WIFE	BYRDE		Johane			Daughter	{				husband's father

MARRIAGE	solemnised at		Marriage		Dates				Remarriage	
no. 237	Colyton		rank of	age at	marriage 21-1-1570	end of union 27-4-1601	length 31	Age at end of union 31-8-1601	NEWTON 599	
	born at	t.p.	residing at	t.p.	baptism	burial	age	Widowhood (months)	buried at	t.p.
HUSBAND					3-1-1544	16-4-1611	67	57	4	
WIFE		t.p.		t.p.	7-1-1548	27-4-1601	53			t.p.

Age groups	Years married	No. of births	Age of mother	Inter-val (months)	sex	rank	Baptisms date	Burials date	status	age	Marriages date	age	Name(s)	Surname of spouse
15–19			22	6	F	1	21-7-1570						Katren	
20–24	25	2	24	18	F	2	27-1-1572						Anne	
25–29	5	2	27	39	F	3	22-5-1575	16-5-1627	wid.	51	7-3-1603	27	Agnes	SCARRE 620
30–34	5	3	29	21	M	4	28-2-1574						Rychard	
35–39	5	2	31	25	M	5	17-4-1579	14-5-1579	s.	28d			Henry	
40–44	5	2	32	10	F	6	2-3-1580						Elsabethe	
45–49	5	0	34	26	F	7	27-5-1582	31-8-1602	s.	20			Charythe	
TOTAL		11	36	28	F	8	16-10-1584	27-10-1584	s.	11d			Sythe	
boys		4	38	18	F	9	24-4-1586	2-3-1663	s.	76			Eddythe	
girls		7	40	31	M	10	15-12-1588						Henry	
Remarks # Melder			43	33	M	11	28-9-1591	2-12-1658	wid.	67	5-6-1615 27-5-1632	23 40	Edward	SALTER 817 HAYMAN 1053
						12								
						13								
						14								
						15								

FRF ii 65

Figure 3·6 Salomon Bird's family (an example of family reconstitution).

85

HUSBAND	BIRD	Salomon	Son	Thomas / Rawlyn		Occupation	
	surname	*name(s)*				husband *weaver*	
WIFE	DOWNE	Agnes	Daughter			husband's father	
						wife's father	

MARRIAGE	*solemnised at*		Marriage		Dates				Age at end of union	Remarriage	
no. **890**	Colyton		rank of	age at	*marriage* 24-1-1620	*end of union* 23-7-1646	*length* 26				
	born at t.p.	*residing at*			*baptism*	*burial*	*age*			Widowhood *(months)*	*buried at* t.p.
HUSBAND	X	t.p.		30	3-2-1589	5-8-1646	57	57			
WIFE	t.p.	X t.p.				23-7-1646					t.p.

Age groups	Years married	No. of births	Age of mother	Inter-val (months)	sex	rank	Baptisms date	Burials date	status	age	Marriages date	age	Name(s)	Surname of spouse
15 – 19				4	F	1	11-6-1620				30-9-1641	21	Rawlyn	ROST 892
20 – 24				21	M	2	25-3-1622	15-8-1641	s.	19			Robert	
25 – 29				33	M	3	16-1-1625	3-8-1646	s.	21			John	
30 – 34				33	M	4	19-10-1627	3-8-1646	s.	18			George	
35 – 39				33	F	5	8-8-1630	30-8-1630	s.	22			Marie	
40 – 44				14	M	6	9-10-1631	2-8-1646	s.	14			Thomas	
45 – 49						7								
TOTAL						8								
boys						9								
girls						10								
Remarks						11								
						12								
						13								
						14								
						15								

FRF ii 65

Salomon Bird grew up in Colyton with William Hore's children at the end of the sixteenth century. Like William Hore he was a craftsman, weaving cloth where William had made shoes, but the history of his family shows the sombre side of life in pre-industrial times and its savage unpredictability. Within a fortnight in late July and early August 1646 he, his wife, and their three surviving children living at home followed one another into the Colyton graveyard. Two children had already died, Marie as a tiny baby, Robert as a youth of nineteen. Rawlyn had married five years earlier and moved from the parish. On 23 July Salomon buried his wife Agnes; on 2 and 3 August his three sons, John, George and Thomas. On 5 August Salomon himself was buried. All were victims of the plague.

Records of this sort are the building blocks which, when put together, reveal the demographic structure of the past, and allow this structure to be related to many aspects of economic and social life. If it is true that '. . . family structures in all societies share a special set of characteristics which make family structure a strategic starting point for general social analysis',[17] then the value of family reconstitution, which provides much information about family structure is evident.

Table 3·5 tells in brief the tale of Colyton's demographic history during three eventful centuries. Much of the finer detail of interest in a more detailed examination of these changes is obscured in this summary, but it does show that the fascinating period in which burials often exceeded baptisms was not the result of any single and simple change, but rather the result of a complex of interrelated changes.

Down to the middle of the seventeenth century men and women both married for the first time at about 27. This is quite a late mean age at first marriage for women since so much of the fertile period has already gone by at that age. On the other hand marital fertility was high once marriage had taken place (see also table 3·6 on page 91) and there were many big families with six or more children. Indeed, of all those women who married beneath the age

87

Table 3·5 The changing demography of Colyton

	Age in years at first marriage		Completed family size of women marrying under 30	Expectation of life at birth in years (sexes combined).	
	M	F			
1560–1646	27	27	6·4	1538–1624	43
1647–1719	28	30	4·2	1625–99	37
1720–69	26	27	4·4	1700–74	42
1770–1837	27	25	5·9		

of 30 and who survived in marriage until the age of 45 (survival of the wife to age 45 in marriage defines a completed marriage in the demographic sense), 55 per cent had six or more children. Moreover expectation of life was remarkably high. A child at birth enjoyed expectation of life of over 40 years at this period. Between 1647 and 1719, on the other hand, when the balance of births and deaths had tilted the other way, the pattern had changed in many respects. Women were marrying two-and-a-half years later in life (enough in itself, other things being equal, to reduce family size by about one child per family), and were a couple of years older than their grooms, an unusual and most interesting development. When married their fertility was considerably less. During this period family limitation appears to have been practised in Colyton.[18] This is indicated by the fact that the fertility of women who married young fell off much more sharply in their thirties and early forties than was the case with women who married later in life. Fertility, which in most pre-industrial societies was primarily a function of the age of the woman, became in this period partially a function of length of marriage. Women marrying under 30 produced families of six or more much less frequently than in the previous hundred years. Only about a fifth of the families were in this size range. Furthermore, expectation of life was lower by about six years. Mortality at all ages was higher (except perhaps in the first year of life; infant mortality did not change much), but the change was particularly marked in the age-groups 1–4 and 5–9.

Fertility began to rise and age at marriage and mortality to fall after 1720 though the changes were at first rather slight. Before the end of the eighteenth century, however, age at marriage, fertility and mortality were all back to levels like those of the sixteenth century. In the early nineteenth century women married still earlier. Mean age at first marriage was only 23 by the end of the last main period, and in the 1820s and 1830s brides were about two and a half years younger than their grooms, the 'normal' pattern to modern eyes. With fertility now very high and expectation of life showing no tendency to fall back, the demographic boom conditions of the sixteenth century were repeated in an even more striking form.

The details of Colyton's population history are fascinating. Multiplied a hundredfold and related to changes in English economy and society during these centuries, information of this type can provide a key to many historical puzzles. On the grand scale, through the intimate links between population changes and the possibility of engendering economic growth, it may help greatly in understanding the genesis of the industrial revolution. On quite a different plane it is interesting to learn that pre-marital intercourse was very common in Colyton. About a third of all first children were baptised within eight months of marriage, many of these in the first three months. This suggests teasing questions about the nature of marriage as a social and personal act. Did society, for example, countenance the living together of a couple once a contract of marriage had been concluded? Or again how clear-cut was the distinction between legitimate and illegitimate births, except in the formal, legal sense? In some cases the parents of a child which was legally a bastard later married. How far did society go in distinguishing between such children and those born in marriage but conceived long before? And what should be made of the most marginal case (which sometimes occurred) of a child baptised on the day of its parents' marriage? In this context, however, the essential point is that both the schedules of fertility and mortality in Colyton changed. They changed in a way which accentuated each other's effect on the balance of births and deaths. High fertility and low mortality were associated with each other, and vice versa.

Colyton provides a good example of the importance of new techniques to the study of long-term demographic fluctuations not because it was necessarily typical, but because it shows how wide the range of what might be called the demographic postures of pre-industrial communities might be. It is possible that many parishes in England conformed roughly to the Colyton pattern in the sixteenth and seventeenth centuries, but it does not follow from this that the absence of population growth in, say, the later Middle Ages in England was due to the same combination of fertility and mortality changes. It is quite on the cards, for example, that changes in the schedule of mortality alone might have produced this effect. Certainly there is no reason to suppose that those continental areas which also knew little or no population growth in the later seventeenth and early eighteenth centuries were subject to the same demographic constraints as were to be found at Colyton. Reconstitution studies in France, for example, show no trace of the fertility patterns found in Colyton until the last decade of the eighteenth century. In general they suggest that the fertility schedules changed little before the 1790s and that the renewed population growth in the eighteenth century was due either to falling mortality, or to earlier marriage, or to a combination of the two.

Extra-European populations

This discussion of short- and long-term fluctuations in population
has relied solely upon pre-industrial European material. A discussion restricted to European experience is unsatisfactory but
difficult to avoid, since it is in general true that an accurate knowledge of the demography of populations elsewhere is first possible
only when the traditional society is rapidly weakening under the
influence of western countries. More will be said of these countries
in transition in chapter 6. But it seems appropriate to mention a
few features of extra-European populations in this chapter, particularly where there are major differences between Europe and other
areas.

Pre-industrial populations outside Europe appear to differ from
European populations consistently in one most important respect –
that marriage, for women at least, was almost universal and came
at a very young age. The so-called 'European' marriage pattern (in
which between two-fifths and three-fifths of the women of child-
bearing age 15–44 were unmarried) was restricted to countries in
western, northern and Mediterranean Europe. This pattern, associated both with a high average age at first marriage and with a
significant proportion of women never marrying, was present in
parts of Europe at least as early as the sixteenth century.[19] In
Tuscany it may have been present by the fourteenth century.[20]
When and how this situation first arose is as yet unknown. To solve
the riddle would be a great service to historical demography.

In contrast with the 'European' marriage pattern, in other areas
only a fifth or less of the women of child-bearing age were unmarried. Often the fraction was considerably less than a fifth. It
would be unwise, however, to assume that this necessarily produced
a radically higher schedule of general fertility. This may have been
the case in some instances, and where it was so, by increasing the
equilibrium totals of population implied by the fertility schedules
and so tending to decrease real incomes, it may have had something
to do with the extreme poverty found in many such populations, a

Table 3·6 Age-specific marital fertility rates in pre-industrial populations inside and outside Europe[21] (rates per 1,000 married women)

	15–19	20–4	25–9	30–4	35–9	40–4	45–9
Crulai (France) 1674–1742	320	419	429	355	292	142	10
Colyton (England) 1560–1629	412	467	403	369	302	174	18
Seven districts, Uttar Pradesh (India) 1953–4	146	239	254	226	190	97	
Yunnan (China) 1942	120	173	181	158	145	87	27
Ramanagaram district, Mysore (India) 1950	177	314	264	201	146	24	1

poverty even deeper than that found in pre-industrial Europe. But there is also evidence in many cases that marital fertility was much lower outside Europe. This, especially when accompanied by a lower average age of woman at the birth of the last child, was often sufficient to bring down the general fertility schedule to levels similar to those found in Europe. Table 3·6 shows how wide the variations in marital fertility between European and other pre-industrial populations can be.

Low marital fertility is often associated with particular social customs. In many parts of India, for example, it is customary for brides to return to their parents' houses for long periods during the early years of marriage (so much so that the average interval between the couple beginning to live together and the birth of the

Table 3·7 The make-up of birth intervals on two extreme assumptions (the figures refer to a woman in her twenties)

	1	2
Amenorrhoea	4	16
Interval before new conception	2	4
Time lost because of foetal deaths	1·5	2·5
From conception to birth of child	9	9
Total (in months)	**16·5**	**31·5**

first child is two or three years in parts of rural India).[22] Elsewhere polygynous marriage customs probably have a similar effect.

The size of birth intervals

In this connection it is worth examining in general terms why it is that mean birth intervals (and hence marital fertility) should differ widely quite apart from the practise of contraception, the abstention from intercourse, or the deliberate procuring of abortions.

In the total interval between any two births there must, of course, be a nine month interval on an average between the conception of the new child and its birth, but there are other components of the interval between births which may vary considerably as shown in table 3·7. There is first a period of amenorrhoea immediately after the birth of the last child during which no ovulation takes place and when no new conception can therefore take place. The duration of this period varies in accordance with factors which are not fully understood. It is likely, however, that this period is considerably lengthened by prolonged suckling of the child. It probably varies in length between extreme limits of four and sixteen months in large populations, though of course in individuals the extremes may be much wider. The minimum is one month. In a small percentage of women the interval may exceed two years. When ovulation does begin again a further interval will elapse before a new conception takes place. In some instances, of course, a woman will conceive again during the first ovulatory cycle but in any large population the average interval will be longer than one month and will vary in part at least as a function of the frequency of sexual intercourse. Here as in so many other matters bearing on fertility the empirical evidence is scanty. Perhaps an intercourse frequency of ten per month for women in their twenties is close to the mean but the range may well be between five and fifteen. In Lebanon among uneducated village Moslems the median frequency of intercourse has been reported as 24·5 occasions per month during the first year of marriage (it is sometimes said that in the Arab world in general the frequency of intercourse is higher than elsewhere).

Two points about intercourse frequency, however, do seem clear; that the frequency varies between different societies by a factor of at least two; and that in all societies the frequency of intercourse declines with age, being only about half as great at forty as at twenty. This factor may add between two and four months to the interval between births in different populations.[23]

Finally, one must add to the other components of the interval between births a figure to express the delay caused by spontaneous abortion. This will consist in turn of the period during which the foetus was carried, a period of temporary infertility after its loss, and a period before renewed conception. In total this is unlikely to be less than five months and may be as high as eight according to the characteristics of different populations. If it is assumed that about a third of all conceptions end in a foetal death (once more the evidence is scant) this may add from, say, $1\frac{1}{2}$ to $2\frac{1}{2}$ months to the average interval between births on opposing extreme hypotheses.

If the various factors are added together, a wide range of possible mean birth intervals result. The lowest total in table 3·7 is 16·5 months. This is almost certainly too low for any large population at any time, for all the components would have to be very favourable simultaneously to produce this figure, which is extremely unlikely. The lowest figures observed, for example in seventeenth-century French Canada (23 months), or in parts of eighteenth-century Flanders (20–23), or in the Hutterite community in the United States in recent decades (about 21 months), are all considerably higher than this.[24] These figures are for women in their early twenties, the period of maximum fertility (the minimum and maximum estimates given in table 3·7 relate to women of this age too) and must, of course, be lower than the average interval for the whole population to which they refer because as age advances all the components of the interval between births except gestation grow larger. The upper limit figure of 31·5 months is also too low. Many populations which do not practise either abortion or contraception have much longer intervals, often in the range 35–50 months for women in this age-group. The reason for this discrepancy must lie in our inadequate understanding of the components of the total interval. For example, it may be that the proportion of ovulatory cycles in which conception cannot take place because the egg is not fecundable may be quite high in some populations (perhaps in all) and may vary widely (perhaps in accordance with the nature of the diet). It can be shown that large variations in this factor would affect the mean interval between births considerably and it is possible that this may explain the big differences in mean birth intervals which have been observed.

Clearly considerable long-term changes in fertility may occur in any population as a result of changes in the birth interval components just described. This is perhaps especially likely to happen as a result of changes in the conventional period of suckling (see pages 123–4). In a fuller discussion several additional factors should be taken into account, notably in populations in which abortions are procured or contraception is practised. Some of these further points are taken up in the next chapter where the social controls upon fertility in pre-industrial European populations are discussed.

Other features

It is convenient before concluding this chapter to mention a number of background features of pre-industrial populations. These features were not cyclical in nature like the short- and long-term fluctuations discussed earlier but they formed a part of the general demographic constitution of these societies and fall into place naturally in this context.

The most important general feature of this sort was the notable difference between the town and the country. When William Farr was investigating the lamentably wide range of expectations of life to be found in different parts of England in the middle of the nineteenth century he attempted to generalise his observations into the empirical law that the mortality of populations in towns varied as the sixth root of the population densities.[25] Whether or not this was a valid generalisation, it does point to a demographic truth of importance – that before the industrial revolution had produced the wealth, and advances in medicine and public health the techniques, to control or eradicate the causes of heavier mortality in towns, life in large settlements was apt to be shorter if less solitary than in the countryside. Poverty, nastiness and brutishness, to complete Hobbes' list, may well have been roughly equally distributed. Where public hygiene and sanitation are absent or misguided the effect on populations scattered in small groups numbering only a few scores or hundreds may be relatively slight, but when people live cheek by jowl in their thousands it creates conditions in which diseases of all types can flourish. In particular some types of epidemic disease spread much more easily in towns and cities. The constant movement of people into and out of cities in the course of administration and trade also served to increase the risk of infection. In some areas of Europe these dangers of urban life were compounded by the danger that when the harvest failed those who lived in the city and were dependent entirely on their money earnings for their livelihood would be worse affected by the shortage and high price of grain than most country dwellers who might either have holdings of their own and so a source of food supply under their own control, or could more easily eke out their supplies of food with gleanings from the hedgerow, common, wood and open field.

To some of these rather sweeping generalisations there were probably important exceptions. Where townsmen were in the main wealthier than countrymen they might be quite well able to draw in food supplies in times of shortage, especially since access to other areas where food was less short was normally easier for a town (which was often situated on navigable water) than for the country. In some areas the political dominance of the city reinforced this advantage, as in Italy in the sixteenth century in times of dearth, famine and plague.[26] Nevertheless it was commonly true that the demography of the towns was quite different from the countryside; that this was increasingly clear as the size of the town increased; and that in most cases mortality rates were considerably higher in the towns.

In England in the sixteenth and seventeenth centuries, for example, plague epidemics were common in the large towns like London, Norwich and Bristol, and each major outbreak brought a very severe toll of life. In London in 1603 at least 33,000 people died of the plague and 10,000 of other causes making a total of 43,000; in the plague of 1625 41,000 (63,000); in the Great Plague of 1665 (the last major English outbreak) 69,000 (97,000).[27] These figures are based on the Bills of Mortality and are minima; the true figures must have been higher and may have been very much higher. In between the big outbreaks there were many years in which plague deaths could be measured by the thousand. During the period 1600 to 1660 the population of London grew from about 200,000 to about 450,000. In plague years therefore between a sixth and a quarter of the population of a great city might die even in the seventeenth century (see also figure 4·1). Yet in many rural parishes the entire period passed without a single plague death, or at any rate without any burst of mortality from plague sufficient to affect the relatively placid graph of deaths year by year (see figure 3·2 on pages 72–3). Not all diseases produced a difference between town and country as clear cut as this, but it is probably true of most of the major killers that the chances of contracting the disease and subsequently dying from it were greater in the town than in the country.

It is less easy to be sure about the fertility characteristics of towns and any systematic differences which may have existed between town and country, but the simple totals of births and deaths make it clear in many cases that urban populations only held their own by immigration. With crude death rates frequently running up to 50 per 1,000 or more it is easy to appreciate this (the London death rate in the gin drinking period of the early eighteenth century may have been as high as 80 per 1,000 in the worst decades). Put differently, in considering the total demographic balance of a pre-industrial society which had developed economically to the point of maintaining towns with populations measured in tens, or even occasionally in hundreds of thousands, it is important to remember that surpluses of baptisms had to exist in rural areas to counter-balance the deficits in the larger towns and cities. If in addition there was a marked growth in city populations the rural surplus had to be so much the larger if the population of the country as a whole were not to decline. The size of London by the later seventeenth and early eighteenth centuries and its continued strong growth in numbers may be estimated to imply that about 8,000 new immigrants (net) came to the city each year. In the demographic conditions of the rest of England at that time this means that London probably absorbed the entire natural increase of a population of two millions or more. This is not only interesting because of the size of the migratory flow, but also because it gives a clue to London's role in furthering social and economic change in late pre-industrial England (see below pages 148–50).[28] In this London was exceptional. Very often the pre-industrial city was not in any way a dynamo driving on the process of change but rather a means of confirming existing attitudes and power structures.[29] London's demographic characteristics, however, may well have been typical of city life until recently, with urban populations maintained only by a steady drift of young men and women in from the countryside.[30]

The contrast between town and country can be illustrated in a different way by drawing what might be called a demographic contour map. This map is built up by drawing lines joining together places with the same average annual rate of natural increase. Over large tracts of the countryside plateau-like conditions might obtain (subject of course to the violent short term fluctuations already described). There might be some areas characterised by rather higher rates of increase than others – for example, areas of stable, mixed farming may for the purpose of this model-map be assumed to show higher surpluses of births over deaths than areas heavily dependent on the unpredictable cereal harvest alone – but in general differences might well be slight. In contrast there would be small areas of very steeply contoured ground where most of the surface was below 'sea-level', in this case the point of balance between births and deaths.

An imaginary map of this sort is reproduced as figure 3·7. On it the unhealthiness of the seaport, and to a lesser extent of the market and the marshland areas, is evident from the contours. The mixed farming area is healthier than the area dependent chiefly on the vagaries of the wheat crop. The map could, of course, be redrawn with the size of each different area made proportional to its population, in which case the seaport's negative balance would loom much larger. If the relative proportions of the urban and rural populations are to be maintained there must be a constant movement of population from the 'higher ground' down into the urban areas and the malarial marshlands. The surface as a whole may be in rough balance (births equalling deaths on a national or regional scale), and the schedules of fertility and mortality for the country as a whole may conform to one of the models described previously, but it is well to bear in mind the possibility that within this overall balance there were notable contrasts between town and country.

It is perhaps worth stressing that there were often rural areas in which the only major industry was agriculture which were nevertheless most unhealthy in pre-industrial times for reasons which had

Figure 3·7 A demographic contour map :
showing how areas of different economic type
might have quite different demographic
characteristics (the figures on the contours
show rates of natural increase or decrease
per 1000 total population).

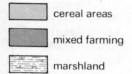

cereal areas

mixed farming

marshland

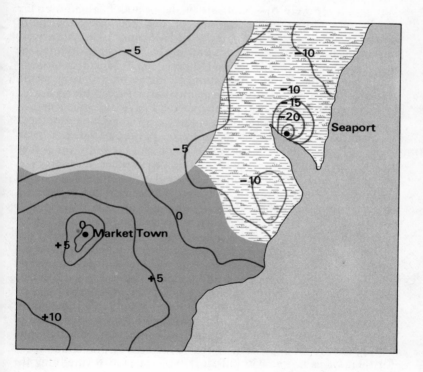

nothing to do with overcrowding on the land. This was especially true of low-lying badly drained areas, where tuberculosis, typhoid and perhaps malaria were difficult to avoid. Drainage in these areas sometimes worked wonders. Contemporaries knew this well. The eighteenth-century doctor Thomas Short claimed that in the Isle of Ely before effective drainage baptisms stood to burials as 61/70: after drainage as 60/54.[31] In the tiny Lincolnshire marsh parish of Wrangle there were 654 baptisms in the period 1704–33 and 173 deaths of children under the age of one producing an infant mortality rate of 265 per 1,000. In 1735 and 1736 there were important local drainage works and in the next three decades the infant mortality rate fell to only 169 per 1,000.[32] Mortality at other ages also declined and expectation of life improved as a result. Areas of this sort could hold their own only if fresh blood flowed into the parish. Without it, numbers would have dwindled steadily.

It is hazardous but perhaps essential to say something too about another feature of the demography of pre-industrial European societies – the differences between the rich and the poor, the gentry and the peasantry, the upper and lower reaches of the social pyramid. The evidence required for a balanced and solidly based analysis is still lacking, and even if the evidence were more plentiful, generalisation might be difficult because the many countries possessed so few common features. But it is a matter of such great interest that some comment is called for.

One way of tackling the question is to erect models which might represent typical cases. Such models will frequently need to be modified or even abandoned altogether in work on a particular society, but they have the advantage of serving as a measuring rod when reviewing facts about some one country and time. It may be of value to outline one such model before going on to make use of information drawn from some empirical studies of this question.

Suppose for example that those whose wealth made it possible for their wives to live without working were guided chiefly by the wish to acquire as a wife someone who was sexually agreeable and therefore young in years. No doubt she would also have to bring with her a suitable dowry or other similar benefits but the two requirements might often be met in the same person. The peasant on the other hand needed a wife who was well versed in domestic and farmyard management (which she might only achieve by a period of service in the household of a substantial yeoman or farmer), and who had had an opportunity to acquire by her own efforts and earnings the domestic utensils and 'bottom drawer' needed to set up house. Where, in order to marry, the peasant needed to acquire land or to be confirmed in the possession of land, and therefore to secure the approval of the owner of the land, the landowner too might well have a strong interest that the man's bride should possess these attributes. In the case of the small free-holder the son's parents in seeking to arrange a match might also think along the same lines. In addition, to a young man in these circumstances the attraction of an older woman, often a widow, who held land in her own right, might far outweigh any considerations falling under the general head of the romantic or sexual. Occasionally a man in straitened circumstances in rural society when contemplating marriage may even have borne in mind the likelihood that a girl in her later twenties would probably bear him fewer children than one in her teens. It may also be assumed in this model that the eldest sons and daughters stood a better chance of marrying early than their brothers and sisters; and that in general the probability of marrying late in life or of remaining celibate rose with rank in the family, the second son or daughter being less likely to marry young than the first.

This model implies, other things being equal, that fertility will be higher towards the apex of the social pyramid because there women marry younger. The differential may be increased if the wealthy employ wet nurses to relieve their wives of the burden of suckling and increase thereby the likelihood that they will quickly become pregnant again (this appears to have happened in Geneva in the early seventeenth century – see page 120 below). On the other hand, these groups often adopted family limitation practices long before the general population.

Other features can be added to the model. To be wealthy is to be well fed even in times of general dearth. The diets of the rich were often badly balanced, and over-eating, especially if accompanied by excessive drinking, sometimes caused ill health and early death. But expectation of life was probably normally better among the upper ranks of society than among the lower. The former could not escape easily in serious epidemic outbreaks (except by flight, and even then their wealth was a notable advantage), but they were largely cushioned from the shock of harvest failure and famine prices which caused the death of so many less fortunate men and women. Moreover a well-fed man is less likely to succumb to infection than a man weakened by short commons over many months. Therefore as a gross generalisation it would be true that mortality rose at each step down the social hierarchy.

It follows from the assumptions of this model that if the proportions of the total population in each social group changed little, social mobility would be chiefly downwards. A combination of higher fertility and lower mortality in the upper reaches of society must tend to produce this effect. It is, of course, a simple matter to produce other models of differential fertility and mortality within a society which have quite different implications for social mobility or for any other aspect of social functioning where the demography of the social groups involved is interlinked with their other activities and beliefs. Malthus, for example, was inclined to make opposite assumptions about fertility by social class because he thought men in the middle and upper classes more likely to be guided by prudential considerations in contemplating matrimony.

When we turn from the comparative simplicity of the model to the complexity of particular historical situations, both the value and limitations of model building may become clearer.

Hedmark in Norway was a rich agricultural area on the shores of Lake Mjoesa where in the early nineteenth century the farming population consisted of two sharply distinct groups – the comparatively wealthy farmers and the crofters who were their tenants at will and whose circumstances were seldom easy. Table 3·8 shows

Table 3·8 Marriage patterns in Hedmark in 1801[33]
(the figures are percentages)

Years older	1–4	5–9	10–14	15 plus	All ages	
Farmers						
Husband	23·0	26·6	14·2	6·5	70·3	Husband on
Wife	13·2	7·1	1·9	0·4	22·6	average 4·4 years older than wife
Crofters						
Husband	19·5	17·7	5·9	3·3	46·4	Husband on
Wife	23·9	14·7	6·1	2·8	47·5	average 0·2 years older than wife

Note the remaining marriages were between partners of the same age. All marriages in the table were between partners never previously married.

how different were the marriage patterns of the two groups. The husbands' ages at first marriage were much the same in both groups, but whereas the farmers were on an average about four and a half years older than their wives, the crofters took as brides women who were much the same age as themselves. Three times as many farmers married women younger than themselves as the reverse, but among the crofters there were slightly more brides older than their grooms than vice versa.

This example conforms quite well to the first model. Other cases, however, though they may show resemblances to the Hedmark case will often differ in important respects. A greatly modified conceptual model is needed to do them justice. A study of the Ting Hsien area of China made in the 1920s, for instance, showed that, as in Hedmark, brides in marriages between wealthy families were younger than those from the poorer sections of the community. In a sample of 766 marriages the wife was older than her husband in

Table 3·9 Mean age at first marriage of British peers and their brides (in years). [34]

Period	M	F	Period	M	F
1575—99	26·3	20·7	1700—24	29·9	23·7
1600—24	26·8	21·4	1725—49	29·4	24·3
1625—49	27·6	22·4	1750—74	29·6	24·0
1650—74	27·5	22·2	1775—99	29·2	25·5
1675—99	28·4	23·0			

70 per cent of the case; in 5 per cent they were the same age; while in only 25 per cent was the husband older. But in Ting Hsien, unlike Hedmark, this was not a phenomenon linked to poverty. On the contrary, the pattern was universal with age at marriage for both brides and grooms inversely correlated with the size of the family holding. The larger the plot, the lower the age at marriage. Families attached great importance to securing the male line at the earliest possible moment. Wealthy families could afford the bride price for their sons and married them off in their early teens to a rather older girl. Poorer families had to wait longer.[35] Hedmark and Ting Hsien may seem to sit oddly together even in the most accommodating model. Traditional China and pre-industrial Europe were far apart culturally as well as in miles. Yet even in a comparison of this sort a model has its uses for it reminds us that because of the link between wealth and age at marriage for women we should examine carefully the possibility that the prevalent drift of social mobility might be downward. If the families of the wealthier groups are larger than average because wives marry younger, their reproduction rates will be higher, and this will be

accentuated if death rates are lower in the upper classes. In these circumstances more people will move down the social ladder than up, if the proportion of the total population in the higher classes is not to rise.

Not only were the demographic characteristics of social groups very different in different societies, they could also change within a single society as time passed. This is well shown by the demographic history of the British peerage. Table 3·9 shows that the average age at first marriage of brides of British peers was very low at the end of the sixteenth century, almost certainly well below the national average at that time (more than six years less than at Colyton, for example). By the end of the eighteenth century a long-sustained and remarkably smooth rise had increased the average by five years to about the level then prevailing in Colyton, and probably slightly above the national average. Grooms showed a similar pattern, though it was somewhat less pronounced. The rise in this case was about three years over the same two centuries, from a figure similar to Colyton's to a substantially higher figure (see table 3·5 on page 87).

The peers always preserved a considerable age-gap between themselves and their brides. It was never less than four years before the last quarter of the eighteenth century. In Colyton, on the other hand, it will be remembered that this changed greatly between the sixteenth and nineteenth centuries, beginning with a period of a century in which grooms and brides were of the same average age, passing through a period when brides were normally older than their grooms, and concluding with the more 'normal' situation with grooms older at first marriage than brides. In the period 1647–1719, in as many as 55 per cent of the marriages the woman was the older party, in 40 per cent the man, and in 5 per cent they were of the same age. By 1800–37 the percentages were 29, 59 and 12 respectively.[36] It is too early to say how typical the changes in Colyton were. They may have been most unusual. But they suggest great caution in generalising not only about differences in age at marriage between different groups within the population, but also about the age-gaps between marriage partners. Comparisons of peers and the inhabitants of Colyton made at different points in time would suggest quite different conclusions on this point.

No demographic model which seeks to show something of the complexity of the relationships between the demographic characteristics and other social and economic features of a society can be successful unless it does justice to the peculiarities of place and time. The foregoing examples of marriage patterns make this very evident. Each set of demographic characteristics arises in its own social and economic setting. Now that the nature of the more important short and long term demographic fluctuations which took place in pre-industrial societies have been examined, and some other general aspects of their population history discussed, it is time to turn to this issue.

4 Society and economy in pre-industrial populations

4 Society and economy in pre-industrial populations

The discussion of population totals in chapter 2 will already have made it clear that the relationships between a society's demography and its economic and social structure are very intricate. This is true both of the functioning of the system of relationships at a given point in time, and still more of the process of change. We should, therefore, be wary about any explanation of these relationships which is claimed to have a universal validity. Any satisfactory analysis of one society at a particular period of its history is likely *ipso facto* to have only a limited value for other societies and periods. It is so difficult to weigh the many variables which must be entertained in the analysis, so difficult in many cases simply to enumerate them, that a full and final analysis of these relationships is likely to continue to elude investigation.

This is not meant as a counsel against attempts to frame models of the interaction of these variables. Indeed, there has been much too little activity of this type in the past. But it is wise to be suspicious of any treatment of these relationships which purports to have solved matters simply by bringing them under a single general head of analysis, such as the view that all population changes occur in the long term in response to changes in the demand for labour.

Possible views of the total situation

A first step in the discussion of this topic is to construct a flow chart showing one possible system of relationships. This helps to bring out the general nature of the variables involved and how they may be related. Figure 4·1 shows a very simple model situation. The existence of a line connecting any two boxes shows that the two phenomena are connected. The direction of the arrow shows the direction of the connection. A plus sign indicates that the relationship is positive; a minus sign that it is negative. Thus box 1 (real income per head) is connected to box 7 (demand for industrial goods) by an arrow with a positive sign, indicating that as real incomes rise they increase the demand for industrial goods. This in turn increases the proportion of the population living in towns

Figure 4·1 A hypothetical model of relationships between demographic, social and economic change.

109

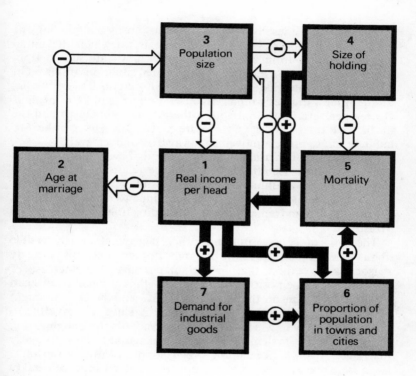

(7–6). As this proportion rises death rates also rise (6–5). Rising death rates are negatively related to population size (5–3), and since there is a negative relationship also between population size and real incomes per head (3–1), the effect of this chain of circumstances is to reinforce the rise in real incomes. However, another chain of circumstances (1–2–3) works in the opposite direction, since it implies that when real incomes per head rise, they push down average age at marriage, causing population to increase and so tending to depress real incomes once more.

The second of these two sets of relationships is the familiar one of negative feedback – a situation, that is, in which the initial movement away from an existing equilibrium state sets in train processes which cause a return to the original situation. If this set of conditions operated independently and fully described the situation, all the three variables would oscillate round a mean level much as the temperature in a room with a thermostat oscillates round the mean, each rise or fall in temperature causing the source of heat to cut in or out to prevent movement away from the set level.

The first set of relationships, however, is one of positive feedback, if taken in isolation. Assuming the relationships remained unchanged over an infinite range of possible levels, once real incomes had begun to rise they would continue to do so indefinitely. Equally, a first movement in the other direction would never be arrested.

There is, of course, nothing either sacrosanct or irreversible about some of the signs in the diagram. For example, it is perfectly reasonable to expect that in certain circumstances increase of population will be positively correlated with real income per head (changing the sign on the arrow between 3 and 1). Or one might plausibly change the sign between 1 and 2, since it is possible to imagine a society in which rising living standards by changing, say, the educational system might also change attitudes to early marriage. Again a population which adopts contraception on a large scale may well begin to marry earlier but yet because fertility falls drastically, the previous relationship between age at marriage and population size will be reversed (2–3). Or the relationship may cease to be either positive or negative. Nowadays, for example, a rising proportion of the population living in cities means neither a higher nor a lower general mortality level since urban living is only marginally more or less healthy than life in the countryside.

Figure 4·1 covers only a few of the variables which were important in pre-industrial societies, and many of these are shown only in a very summary form and could themselves be broken down into sub-systems. For example, the relationship between population size and real incomes per head (3–2), even though it may hold good for a population as a whole in a particular historical setting, may conceal differences between classes which were of crucial significance at that juncture. Periods when the peasantry were oppressed by the weight of their own numbers were often periods of splendid prosperity for those who owned the land.

In one vital respect pre-industrial societies were by definition in a position of negative feedback. Each period of economic growth was eventually cut short before reaching the point at which it was self-sustained and progressive. The period of industrial revolution is that period in which this restriction is overcome, in which the whole system of relationships between population, economy and society is so changed that the process of growth no longer sets up barriers to its own further progress (an example of this removal of a negative feedback situation will be found on pages 56–9 above where the change in raw material supply to industry from organic to inorganic materials is described). This issue is taken up again in the next chapter.

If the relationships between population, society and economy are approached along the lines suggested by the model in figure 4·1, there is no one point of entry into the system which is necessarily better than another. The decision to choose one rather than another is arbitrary and will reflect the particular purposes of the moment. In this instance it is perhaps convenient to begin with the question of population size.

In pre-industrial populations the total effect of the interplay of demographic with other variables was to preserve a rough balance between births and deaths. There were, of course, periods of population growth, and the trend of numbers on a very long view was upwards, but the rate of growth was slight overall and long-term trends were often almost blotted out by the amplitude of short-term fluctuations. In a sense, of course, a balance between births and deaths was bound to be preserved in the general case because the schedules of fertility and mortality plotted against population size were certain to cross at some point as the result of the existence of a 'ceiling' (see figure 2·1 on page 34). In the limiting case this might be because of the operation of positive checks alone as Malthus envisaged in his gloomiest moments. But we have already seen that the worst seldom if ever happened. More commonly societies adopted modes of behaviour which reduced fertility in such a way as to produce a point of balance between births and deaths some way short of the maximum possible.

Instances of this social control of numbers have already been given in chapter 2. In many primitive cultures a type of negative feedback system operated over family size. The fact of the existence of earlier children in a family decreased the likelihood that a new conception would take place, or that having taken place it would go to term, or that having been born it would be allowed to live, according to the method of control locally employed. Each addition to a family darkened the prospects of the next child. Sometimes the pressure exerted by society upon its members might take account not only of the circumstances of the individual family but of the tribe as a whole, as when the elders of the Australian Wadthawing tribe decided the fate of a new-born child. It seems reasonable to suggest that the effect of the existence of regulation of this type was to produce population totals close to the optimum given the circumstances of primitive economy and society. It is also reasonable to suppose that such systems arose over many generations as a result of a degree of social selection which favoured tribes which developed more sensitive methods of achieving this. Wynne-Edwards in discussing animal populations uses the idea of population homeostasis:

To build up and preserve a favourable balance between population density and available resources, it would be necessary for the animals to evolve a control system in many respects analogous to the physiological systems that regulate the internal environment of the body and adjust it to meet changing needs. Such systems are said to be homeostatic or self-balancing . . . .[1]

This concept, which has close links with that of negative feedback, is also sometimes helpful in considering pre-industrial societies.

The typical cycle of events during a demographic crisis in the peasant areas of western Europe before the industrial revolution is an example of <u>homeostatic adjustment</u>. When harvests were bad marriages were postponed and the number of conceptions fell very sharply indeed just at the time when burials rose to a peak (see figure 3·1) – complementary trends which might reduce the population by a quarter in a couple of years and so bring food supplies more nearly into balance with the number of mouths to be fed. Conversely, when normal harvests were again available, not only did mortality drop to a level well below average (because the most vulnerable members of the population had died during the food crisis), but the number of births rose sharply because many postponed marriages were now celebrated and parents were once more willing to add to their families. As a result populations often recovered their former size in a further decade. No pre-industrial society was able entirely to escape from the demographic rhythm imposed by fluctuating food supplies, but some succeeded in avoiding the worst dangers associated with fluctuations of this type by developing schedules of fertility low enough to ensure that the population totals reached were sufficiently small to avoid a great pressure of population upon the food base. In these societies a smaller fraction of the population lived balanced on the edge of a Malthusian precipice. This might be called long-term homeostatic adjustment in contrast to the short term changes just described. Societies which succeeded in this respect may also have been those best able to make further advances in material technology and so to raise eventually both population totals and the standards of living attainable. If this were so they would enjoy a selective advantage in competition with other societies whose exuberant fertility denied them these opportunities.

It is interesting to note, incidentally, as evidence of the nature of demographic changes which might be called homeostatic, that the typical changes occurring during a period of severe epidemic mortality were quite different from those in which the root problem was food shortage, even though the death rates were at comparable

Table 4·1 Plague epidemics in London[2] and in three Norwich parishes

London				3 Norwich parishes†		
Year	Total buried	Died of plague	Baptisms	Year	Burials	Baptisms
1622	8,959	16	7,894	1575	55	74
1623	11,112	17	7,945	1576	38	83
1624	12,210	11	8,299	1577	38	87
1625	54,265	35,417*	6,983	1578	40	78
1626	7,535	134	6,701	1579	561	74
1627	7,715	4	8,408	1580	82	82
1628	7,743	3	8,564	1581	44	106
				1582	42	72
				1583	53	91

* This figure is smaller than that given on page 96 because it excludes outlying London parishes like Stepney, Newington and Lambeth.

† St Stephen, St Andrew, St Peter Mancroft.

Death thru epidemics + starvations } caused diff. demogr. changes

levels. In the latter case as the death rate shot up the number of conceptions taking place declined remarkably; in the former the changes on the fertility side were much slighter. If the number of births fell, it was normally only a modest fall, related probably to the deaths of pregnant mothers, to abortions brought on by severe illness, and to panic flight of part of the population away from the seat of infection. Even during the most severe of plague outbreaks the number of births usually held up surprisingly well. Table 4·1 illustrates this point from the Norwich plague of 1579 and the London plague of 1625. The London figures of burials and baptisms are known to be less than the true figures of deaths and births but, unless there was a change in the degree of under-registration, this does not reduce the value of the evidence for the present purpose. The peak mortality from plague normally occurred in the autumn and therefore any effect on the conception rate would be reflected in the baptism figures for the following year, though the death or illness of pregnant women might cause an earlier dip in baptisms also. It will be seen that in the Norwich parishes the enormous loss of life (probably a full third of the population) had no effect on the baptism rate, presumably both because the fertility of the survivors was very little changed and because immigrants flooded in to take the places of the plague victims. There was a surge of marriages after the plague but no preceding period in which marriages almost ceased. The contrast with, say, the Beauvaisis parish of Mouy in table 3·1 is very marked. In London the impact of the plague on baptisms is certainly visible but the fall in the total of baptisms is no larger than the fall in total population which must have occurred, and again the rapidity of full recovery is very noticeable. Where the logic of the situation, as it were, required a shrinkage in total numbers, marriages and births fell abruptly. Where on the contrary the high mortality came by the arbitrary incidence of an epidemic, no such change in the level of marriages and births was called for.

Demographic characteristics

So far only ways of conceiving the general system of relationships affecting pre-industrial demography have been discussed. It is now convenient to turn to the various elements which together made up these demographic systems and to discuss some of the ways in which economic and sociological circumstances affected them or were affected by them.

1 Age at marriage and fertility One need hardly emphasise the importance of this variable to the fertility levels of any community which does not practise control of fertility within marriage. In such communities the fertility of women is mainly a function of their age. If therefore they spend many of their child-bearing years outside marriage, much reproductive potential is permanently lost. Other things being equal this in itself can result in total fertility levels which differ from each other by a factor of two between a community in which the average age at first marriage is the very early twenties and another where it is about 30. In pre-industrial European communities a range of this size can be shown to have occurred. This immediately raises the possibility of substantially different population totals and levels of real income in relation to any given economic base (following the argument of chapter 2). If as population density rises a community adjusts to the attendant problems by raising the average age at first marriage, population growth will cease at a lower total than otherwise.

The mere fact that women married at very different ages in different communities draws attention to economic and socio-logical points of great importance (the mean age at first marriage of men is, of course, also very important, but it is much less important demographically since men frequently remain able to procreate into their sixties and sometimes to much greater ages). The act of marriage is necessarily one which stands centrally in the whole complex of social behaviour. The family is a basic unit in all cultures and the creation of a new family by marriage is bound to interest society as a whole as well as the individuals and families most directly involved. Society prescribes norms of conduct and all but a few deviant individuals will conform to them. In many African and Asian societies it was thought shameful that a young girl should remain unmarried once she was sexually mature (often defined as the onset of menstruation). Economic arrangements dovetailed with this attitude by providing that for some years after they were first married a young couple should live in the household of a parent. Later they might acquire a house of their own but inability to purchase or build a house in youth when marriage took place did not mean that the marriage was postponed. Goode remarks of Arab societies that, '. . . the extended family was a stage in the life cycle of the individual and the family unit as well'.[3] With modification this was true of many pre-industrial societies outside Europe.

In pre-industrial western European societies, however, things were very different. Marriage normally meant the creation of a new household immediately and could therefore not take place unless the economic basis for a new household existed. If, to take an extreme example, the stock of houses in a community was fixed (say by the attitude of the landlord to new construction) new families could only be established when an existing house fell vacant. When a three-generation household came into existence it was usually because room was found for an aged father or mother of the married couple rather than because a newly married bride and groom moved in with one of the parental couples. Where this conjunction of sociological, economic and demographic circumstances exists it makes possible the preservation of a given standard of life and permits a flexible adjustment to changed conditions. If, say, there is a rise in child mortality for any reason and some years later a fall in the number of young men and women of marriageable age, then, with a normal flow of marriage opportunities, more than usual of the young adults will be able to marry early; their families will be large; and fertility will have risen to offset the mortality change. The possibility of a system of homeostatic adjustment taking this form does not mean that it can often be discerned in operation. Rather it falls into place as part of the armoury of weapons available to western European societies in the struggle to produce, however unconsciously, effective ways of bringing men and their means of livelihood into balance. Eastern Europe makes an instructive contrast with western Europe here for in the east the extended family was still common (more than one married couple in a household) and women married very young.

Amongst western European populations before the industrial revolution there were many circumstances which tended to keep up the age at marriage. Youths and young girls went out to service in other households in their early teens and spent many years in service in this way. As long as they were servants they were very rarely free to marry, and they could only leave service when they were in a position to establish an independent household by the acquisition or inheritance of land, of a craft workshop, or of a position which made them independent.[4] Apprenticeship, a more formal version of the system of putting out to service in another household, also meant a prolongation of bachelorhood. In some areas it was necessary as a matter of law and in many others as a matter of fact to obtain the permission of the local lord or landowner before marriage. He in turn might hold strong views on the multiplication of holdings, houses and households. It would be difficult in most instances to allot these influences upon age at marriage confidently to an economic or sociological pigeon hole except by rather special pleading. They spring from an amalgam of legal requirements (over permission to marry, or apprenticeship regulations), customary attitudes (which were often firmly adhered to long after the circumstances in which they had originally appeared had vanished), economic necessities (failure to acquire land, or to obtain a house), and social prohibitions (for example, of the existence of more than one family in each household).

An average age at first marriage for women in the mid-twenties would, of course, have meant little if there had been a large number of illegitimate births among unmarried women, and especially if consensual unions of the type often found today in the

West Indies had occurred widely. In general, however, only a tiny fraction of the potential fertility of young unmarried women was released in this way. Illegitimate births did form a surprisingly high proportion of the total in some areas. For example, at Prestbury in Cheshire during the years 1581–1600 the proportion ran as high as 16 per cent (135 out of a total of 876 baptisms performed). And this is a minimum figure since bastards were probably more likely to die in the first hours or days of life than other babies and in these circumstances fail to be baptised. Before the later eighteenth century, however, few English registers show more than one bastard in 20 baptised. Frequently the figure was much lower. In some French parishes the number of illegitimate children baptised was astonishingly small. In Crulai in Normandy, for example, only 20 such baptisms were performed between 1604 and 1699, or 0·6 per cent of all babies baptised.[5]

There is no evidence that exceptionally high mean ages at first marriage were associated with high percentages of illegitimate children. Indeed the reverse relationship was probably more common. Where early marriage was widely countenanced, extra-marital intercourse was often also common and the percentage of illegitimate births rather high, whereas if a community set its face against early marriage illegitimate births were nevertheless usually few in number. The small proportion of illegitimate births does not, of course, rule out the possibility of extensive extra-marital intercourse assuming that effective means of preventing conception or destroying the foetus were known and widely practised, but this would be a very bold assumption on present knowledge.

In pre-industrial Europe the chief means of social control over fertility was by prescribing the circumstances in which marriage was to be permitted. But it would be mistaken to suppose that once marriage had taken place fertility was governed solely by physiological and nutritional factors. Customary practises could continue to have a marked effect on fertility even after marriage had taken place. Henry's path-breaking study of the Genevan bourgeoisie[6] affords ample evidence of this and gives point to the dictum that

Table 4·2 Marital fertility in the Genevan bourgeoisie[7]
(births per 1,000 woman-years lived)

Husband born	Age of woman 15–19	20–4	25–9	30–4	35–9	40–4	45–9
before 1600	264	389	362	327	275	123	19
1600—49	419	525	485	429	287	141	16
1650—99	348	493	400	244	130	35	5

'Population statistics form an appropriate basis for probing into the subtlest nuances of social life'.[8]

Table 4·2 shows the notable changes in age-specific marital fertility which occurred over a period of a century and a half from the mid-sixteenth century. The wives of the Genevan bourgeoisie displayed a fairly high fertility at the time when it is first possible to study this in detail, but fertility increased sharply in the early seventeenth century, only to fall again later in the century when fertility rates in the later age-groups above 30 were very much lower than in either of the earlier periods. The sudden rise in marital fertility after 1600 was accompanied, of course, by a parallel fall in the average interval between births (from 2·44 to 2·06 years in completed families).[9] Direct evidence about the cause of this change is lacking but Henry believes it may have been due to the practise of putting babies out to wet nurse which became normal at about this time. This would eliminate the period of low fecundity associated with suckling and bring down the mean interval between births abruptly.

Larger families mean more dowries to find, more sons to be provided for. Their increased fertility created personal, social and

Table 4·3 Mean birth intervals in Genevan bourgeois completed families of four or more children[10] (in months)

Rank order of birth intervals	Husband born:		
	before 1600	1600–49	1650–99
1–2	28·5	23·5	19·7
2–3	29·4	25·4	21·6
3–4	27·4	23·5	30·1

economic pressures upon the Genevan bourgeoisie. Many more of their sons were obliged to seek their living outside the city. The group had outgrown their ecological niche, and it is not perhaps fanciful to see a close connection between the spurt in marital fertility about 1600 and the adoption of means of controlling fertility within the family half a century later. Even when family limitation was clearly widespread there was no rise in the mean intervals between the early births in the families. Indeed the intervals between the first and second, and the second and third births fell, but thereafter the intervals became much longer, as may be seen in table 4·3. Moreover the age which mothers bore their last child in completed families fell sharply (from 38·5 years before 1650 to 34·3 years 1650–99).[11] Family size shrank steadily from the mid-seventeenth century onwards. The difficulties of raising large families while at the same time maintaining conventional middle-class standards of life have been examined recently for Victorian England. Banks concludes that these problems had much to do with the spread of family limitation among the English middle classes from the 1870s onwards.[12] It is quite possible that similar tensions in seventeenth-century Geneva had a similar result.

Table 4·4 Marital fertility rates in two small areas of France in the eighteenth century[13] (per 1,000 woman-years lived)

	20–4	25–9	30–4	35–9	40–4	45–9
Sainghin-en-Mélantois 1690–1739	512	521	419	402	220	31
Thézels and Saint-Sernin 1700–92	385	335	290	242	67	0

It is obvious that the problem which faced the Genevan bourgeoisie could not arise in the same form for a whole population. Wet nursing cannot in the nature of things be made available to the offspring of all mothers. It is probable, too, that a well-educated bourgeoisie is more likely than other groups in the population to see the connection between size of family and standard of life, and to take steps to overcome difficulties brought on by inconveniently large families when they become pressing. But it would be mistaken to suppose that large variations in marital fertility were restricted to special groups within populations. For example, table 4·4 shows how large were the differences between two small areas of eighteenth-century France. Sainghin-en-Mélantois is in the department of Nord. Thézels and Saint-Sernin are two parishes in Lot in south-west France. The difference in marital fertility between the two parishes is very large. A group of married women whose fertility was at the level of Sainghin-en-Mélantois and who lived in marriage throughout the three decades of child-bearing 20–49 would produce on an average 10·5 children each. The comparable figure for Thézels and Saint-Sernin is only 6·6.

The demographic history of Colyton shows that there might also

Table 4·5 Marital fertility rates in Colyton[14]
(per 1,000 woman-years lived)

	20–4	25–9	30–4	35–9	40–4	45–9
1560–1629	467	403	369	302	174	18
1647–1719	346	395	272	182	104	20

be considerable fluctuations over time within the same parish as appears from table 4·5. The completed family sizes in this case are 8·7 and 6·6 calculated on the same basis as for the French parishes. It is interesting to note, incidentally, that the marital fertility differences in the French parishes were offset by differences in age at marriage which worked in the opposite direction. The average age at first marriage of women in Sainghin-en-Mélantois was 28·9 years; at Thézels and Saint-Sernin only 24·7.[15] A longer period of child-bearing in marriage compensates, of course, for lower fertility rates when the total reproductive effort of a whole generation of women is considered. But in Colyton the fall in marital fertility rates was exaggerated by a rise of about two and a half years in the average age at first marriage of women between the two periods.

How did such large variations in marital fertility occur? Apart from variations due to nutritional or conceivably to genetic differences, there are several important respects in which fertility is socially or individually controlled (though *not*, of course, necessarily as a result of conscious policy). A long suckling period causes prolonged amenorrhoea and so increases the intergenesic interval (the interval between births). In the days before baby foods, rubber teats and feeding bottles children were fed at the breast much longer than is now customary. The pioneer family reconstitution study done upon the parish registers of Crulai showed that whereas the normal interval between two births was 29·6 months, the interval was only 20·7 months when the preceding child died before reaching its first birthday.[16] Henry was able to show that in the great majority of cases this was due to the death of the earlier child permitting a new conception, rather than the new conception increasing the risk to the living child. And subsequent studies have confirmed this point. Where therefore the customary suckling period was short, the intergenesic interval would probably also tend to be short – but unfortunately there is little evidence about the relative lengths of suckling periods.

Where contraception was practised it is probable that the commonest method was *coitus interruptus*. This is thought to have been very widely used in those areas of France in which marital fertility fell steadily at the end of the eighteenth century and in the early decades of the nineteenth.[17] It was much the commonest method used later in the century in the rest of Europe. It is known to have been used in a number of primitive societies (see page 42) and its use has further been suspected in crisis periods in pre-industrial Europe even in communities which may otherwise have eschewed it.[18] Knowledge of the method probably lay at the disposal of European communities throughout the pre-industrial period. There is very strong statistical evidence pointing to the existence of family limitation in Colyton during the late seventeenth and early eighteenth centuries, and *coitus interruptus* appears more likely to have been used than any other method.[19] It has, indeed, been suggested that in general *coitus interruptus* (essentially a male technique) is more likely to have been employed in societies where the conjugal family was the most usual unit, with responsibility for the maintenance of children falling on the father, than in an extended family system where this responsibility was more widely dispersed in a kin group.[20]

The procuring of abortions and infanticide may be treated

together under the general head of means of reducing marital fertility, even though strictly speaking they are rather ways of increasing mortality. Since marital fertility in Europe was in general at a high level it is unlikely that a great many abortions were procured. Yet it is clear that abortions were attempted at times in all populations. The ecclesiastical authorities were worried from time to time about the extent of the problem and it is noteworthy that in England when a Bishop or his chancellor administered the midwife's oath, one injunction read:

You shall not give any counsel, or minister any herb, medicine, or potion, or any other thing, to any woman being with child, whereby she should destroy or cast out that she goeth withal before her time.[21]

Midwives were also required to swear that they would not 'suffer any woman's child to be murdered, maimed, or otherwise hurt . . .'.[22] As a fully conscious, deliberate act infanticide was probably rare in Europe by early modern times, but infanticide is not a clear-cut crime. If one were to include under this head the casual overlaying of children and varying degrees of neglect and ill treatment which contributed to early death the number of victims would appear much greater. Many died as a result of actions by their parents which conformed to the cynical maxim 'Thou shalt not kill but needst not strive officiously to keep alive'. Institutions developed in the large cities which acted in effect if not in formal intention as agencies for the disposal of unwanted children, both legitimate and illegitimate. These sometimes culled far higher percentages of the annual crop of births than practices which we are sometimes pleased to term 'savage', such as the putting to death of all twins.

The *asile* of Saint Vincent de Paul in Paris took in more and more foundlings from the late seventeenth century onwards. By the end of the third quarter of the eighteenth century about a third of all the babies born in Paris found their way there. But very few left. Death rates were so high in institutions of this sort that in the healthiest of them a third or more of those admitted died within a

Figure 4·2 An illustration of the effect of a rise in the mortality schedule on population growth rates and on the equilibrium level of population.

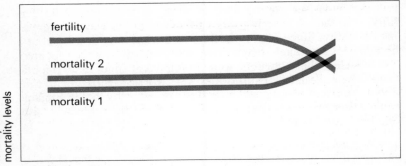

fertility

mortality 2

mortality 1

fertility and mortality levels

population size

year of entry. In the worst the proportion rose to nine-tenths.[23] It was much the same story in London where the foundling hospitals and workhouses have recently been described as 'highly effective infanticide agencies'.[24] The infant death rate in workhouses in 14 London parishes in the eighteenth century was estimated at 88 per cent by a contemporary, Jonas Hanway, who inquired into the matter.[25] That which society condones does not, of course, in general cause much contemporary comment however shocking it may later seem. Viewed coldbloodedly, indeed, infanticide is an efficient method of limiting fertility in that it endangers the health of the mother less than an abortion procured in unhygienic surroundings and need be much less often carried out since a child unfortunate enough to die in this way will have gone to full term, whereas an abortion takes up only a few months of a woman's fertile period.

Contraceptive practices, the procuring of abortions and infanticide were all much more likely to occur in unions outside marriage than within marriage. In this way a stock of knowledge about means of limiting fertility was maintained upon which the married population could draw when choice or necessity caused them to try

to limit fertility. Occasionally the existence of this stock is revealed
in the writings of contemporaries, particularly when they describe
the habits of prostitutes; or may come to light in the records of
ecclesiastical courts. There is an intriguing example of this in a case
presented in the course of the Archibishop of York's Metropolitical
Visitation of the Diocese of Chester in 1590. Edward Shawcross,
vicar of Weaverham in Cheshire, was accused under a number of
heads. His indictment ends with two charges, one common enough,
the other affording a tantalising glimpse of a sexual sub-culture
which only rarely produces a written record:

He is vehementlie suspected for committinge adulterye with dyvers and
sundrie women. He is also an instructor of yoong folkes how to comyt the
syn of adultrie or fornication and not to beget or bring forth children.[26]

2 Mortality Some of the most important influences on mortality
were altogether outside the control of pre-industrial societies. If a
mutation in a virus strain greatly increased the virulence of an
endemic disease, for example, it might substantially alter expectation of life in the society and perhaps its age structure also. For
instance, the incidence of smallpox is peculiarly heavy in the early
years of life (in populations in which it is endemic, though not, of
course, in populations into which it is introduced for the first time
when people of all ages may die in large numbers). Let us assume,
simply by way of illustration, that death from smallpox is confined
to the first year of life and that it kills a twentieth of all children
before they reach their first birthday. If the fatal incidence of the
disease suddenly doubles as a result of an increase in its virulence,
the change which this entails may be seen in figure 4·2. The population will grow more slowly (mortality **2** is closer to the fertility line
than mortality **1**), and if, in other respects, mortality changes in
response to increasing population pressure much as it would otherwise have done, the equilibrium total of population will be smaller
than before. Moreover, there will be an 'ageing' of the population
(see pages 26–8). Alternatively, indeed, the change can be viewed
as a fall of a twentieth in fertility rather than as a rise in mortality

since only the very young are affected (and fertility changes have a marked effect on the age structure of populations). Diseases may disappear as well as grow more common, of course, as with plague in much of Europe in the seventeenth century, and where this occurs the general mortality schedule may be lowered with opposite results to those just described.

Before the late nineteenth century men were not in general able to counter infectious diseases effectively by drawing upon medical knowledge or by public health measures. There is little evidence that medical treatment was able to reduce mortality from the major killing diseases significantly except perhaps at the very end of the pre-industrial period when inoculation against smallpox may have had some effect. Some public health measures may have helped to reduce infection, as, for example, when James I in July 1603 granted a license for plays 'as soon as the plague decreases to 30 deaths per week in London'.[27] But in the main neither doctor nor mayor could turn back the tide of infection. The presence of aromatic herbs in court may have reduced the offence to the judge's nose caused by the fetid persons of the prisoners, but it did not affect his liability to be bitten by a typhus-carrying louse. Nor did the burning of bedding and other household furniture tipped out of plague houses much affect the spread of that terrible disease.

To take refuge in flight was often the most sensible preventive measure which any individual could take at the time of an epidemic, but, though this may have enhanced his own chances of survival, it worsened the chances of the population as a whole since a proportion of those who fled from an infected spot carried the disease with them and so spread it elsewhere. Sir Herbert Croft, a member of the Council of the Marches of Wales in the early seventeenth century, is alleged to have ordered an unfortunate plague victim probably fleeing from elsewhere to be drowned in the Lugg at Leominster.[28] He hastened the poor man's end to prevent the spread of infection. This was perhaps mere panic inhumanity, but in as much as an example of this sort may have discouraged others from doing likewise it would tend to lessen the total mortality.

Queen Elizabeth I went so far as to erect a gallows at Windsor in September 1563 on which to hang anyone who might endanger the health of the court by fleeing thither from London.[29]

If there is little evidence that medical measures saved life, there is equally little evidence that they greatly increased the death rate, however bizarre some methods of treating the patient, except that the herding together of the sick into hospitals increased the likelihood of cross-infection and raised morbidity. This was still a great problem in the early maternity hospitals where deaths among mothers from puerperal fever and among babies from infant ailments occurred on a horrifying scale because the hospital administration of the day was unable to deal with the dangerous infections caused, or at least maintained and multiplied, by proximity.

The inability of pre-industrial societies to protect themselves against disease by medicine and public health measures does not mean that mortality levels were not greatly influenced by social and economic conditions. On the contrary the level of real income enjoyed by a population played a great part in determining its death rate. Abundant food, good clothing and warm dwellings can cause a vast improvement in mortality even when medical knowledge is slight, while conversely those who face the rigours of winter in rags, those who live with their families in damp and chilly hovels or have no shelter at all, are much more likely to fall victim to disease and, having done so, to succumb.

While in general increasing real incomes probably tended to reduce mortality they might also set in train countervailing tendencies since rising real incomes tended also to produce a notable growth in city populations. In the crowded and insanitary conditions prevailing in the cities, not even the possession of higher real incomes could save men and women from the increased danger of infection. Disease is no respecter of wealth unless fat purses can procure the sanitary and medical knowledge necessary to preserve health, and such knowledge did not exist. Playing with ideas, indeed, as figure 4·3 shows, it is possible to imagine a rise in real incomes producing a fall in total population. The higher real incomes, by

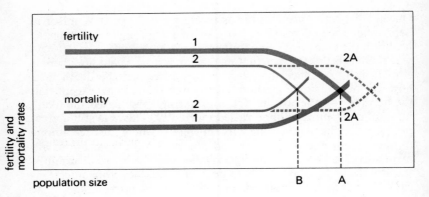

Figure 4·3 An illustration of the possible effects of growing urbanisation upon population size and upon levels of fertility and mortality.

fertility

1

2

2A

mortality

2

1

2A

fertility and mortality rates

population size

B   A

causing a disproportionately steep rise in the demand for industrial products, services and trade goods, may cause a sudden spurt in town growth. If the death rates in towns are very high, the greater productivity attainable by using the new techniques, instead of giving rise to a higher equilibrium population total may well produce a lower one, for the curve expressing mortality will now be higher with a larger fraction of the population living in towns and cities (mortality **2** in figure 4·3).

If at the same time urban fertility rates are lower than those in rural areas the fall in numbers will be exaggerated and population might sink back from **A** to **B** in the hypothetical case shown in figure 4·3. It is, of course, easily possible to imagine quite different results from increasing urbanisation. The fertility and mortality levels marked **2** in the diagram may still hold good, but the equilibrium total be higher than before. The dotted extensions (**2A**) illustrate this. They represent a situation in which the higher productivity achieved by a change in material culture postpones to a larger population total the pressure upon fertility and mortality caused by increasing numbers, and therefore the lines begin to converge later. The population increases more slowly because of unfavourable urban birth and death rates but moves towards a higher total. This may have been the commoner historical situation. The first possibility is not purely theoretical, however. England in the seventeenth and eighteenth centuries shows something of this pattern (see pages 148–51).

Expectation of life at birth may be used as a shorthand expression of death rates at all ages. Combinations of favourable or unfavourable circumstances could result in notable differences in expectation of life even before the benefits of modern medical knowledge were available. Although it is comparatively rare to have accurate information of this sort about pre-industrial European populations, enough exists to show that it could vary very substantially. Duvillard's mortality table for France in the later eighteenth century gives an expectation of life of 28·8 years.[30] In parts of France it must clearly have been less than this. In the great cities, both in France and elsewhere, it was seldom much over 20 years. In Crulai in the period 1675–1775 it was about 30 [31]; in Elizabethan Colyton just over 40; and in the early days of settlement in Plymouth colony in New England there is reason to suppose it may have been as high as 50 years in some places.[32]

The use of models

This brief review of the range of levels of fertility and mortality shows that numbers could rise or fall or remain stationary from an enormous range of combinations of demographic rates. Before examining further the relationship of these rates to economic and social conditions, it may prove interesting to show how assumptions about the nature of a community's demography can improve the judgment of the historical material itself.

Consider, for example, the question of the proportion of households containing grandparents as well as parents and their children. Much is written of the significance of this arrangement as an index of the prevalence of a certain type of familial organisation. But if it is known (say from a listing of inhabitants divided by household) that 15 per cent of all households contained three generations, what can be made of this? Is it a high or a low proportion? To answer the question one must know how often such an arrangement might occur. The number of old people is always too few to permit each household to contain one. But what would constitute a high figure having regard to the number of old people in the community? Examining the properties of a model population will help to answer this question.

It requires only a slight knowledge of the properties of stable populations to know that in societies in which the expectation of life is low and fertility high the proportion of old people in the population must be small. The generation of a model population with an expectation of life of 30 years and a gross reproduction rate of 2·5 (see page 20 for the definition of GRR) shows that the proportion of the population over 60 will be 5·5 per cent. This may be compared with a figure of 13 per cent when expectation of life reaches 70 years with a GRR of 1·5. Clearly the demographic type of the population will have an important bearing on the number of households which are likely to include a grandparent.

Let us assume that we are dealing with a society in which on marriage a young couple begin life together in a separate house or cottage. Let us further assume that the older generation of married couples continue to live together as long as they are both alive but that when one dies the other will always go to live with his or her married son or daughter. In this situation a number of three-generation households will arise, but in order to judge how many such households there might be assuming this convention existed, we must specify the main demographic characteristics of the population and examine the properties of the model further.

Assume that the population is stable and stationary, that the mean age at marriage for both sexes is 27, and that the mean age of married couples is 40. Assume further that the mean age of mothers at which children are born has been stable in this community at 32 for some years. Then the mean age of the parents of married couples will be 72. If the United Nations specimen life table level 25 (expectation of life at birth 32·5 years) is assumed to apply to this population, then the number of people aged 72 will be just under a quarter of the number of their descendants aged 40.[33] A simple binomial expansion shows how likely it is that the household of a married couple will contain a grandparent. There are five possibilities.

1 That all four grandparents are living
2 That three are living and one has died
3 That two are living and two have died
4 That one is living and three have died
5 That all four have died

The expression $(p + q)^4$ where p is the probability of surviving from 40 to 72 ($p = \frac{1}{4}$) shows that the possibilities will occur with the following relative frequencies.

1 Will occur in the proportion 1:256. This will give rise to no three-generation households since no marriage has been broken by death.

2 Will occur in the proportion 12:256. Each instance of this possibility must include one married couple. The third grandparent will live with a married child. But there may be more than one married child to whom he or she can move. It can be shown that the chance of any one married child receiving the grandparent is about 42 in 100 (this figure is derived by a binomial expansion from the assumption that two babies in every five survive to the age of 40 and that family size varies between one and nine with an equal probability of each size occurring). Therefore the chance of three-generation households arising in this way is $\frac{12}{256} \times \frac{42}{100}$, or 2·0 per cent of the total of households.

3 Will occur in the proportion 54:256. In a third of these cases the two survivors will be man and wife and will continue to live together. This leaves 36 cases where the survivors are from different marriages, one related to the husband and one to the wife. There is a $\frac{58}{100} \times \frac{58}{100}$ chance that no grandparent will move to either the

husband or the wife, or approximately $\frac{34}{100}$. In the remainder of the cases $\frac{66}{100}$ a three-generation household will occur. In the total of all households $\frac{36}{256} \times \frac{66}{100}$, or 9·3 per cent will contain three generations because this situation occurs.

4 This is the most likely of the five possibilities and will occur in the proportion 108:256. For the reasons given above a three-generation household will occur in $\frac{108}{256} \times \frac{42}{100}$ cases, or 17·8 per cent of all households.

5 In many cases no grandparents at all survive. Here the proportion is 81:256.

Summing the chances of one or more grandparents living with their children and grandchildren in a three-generation household produces a figure of 29·1 per cent, well under a third of all cases.

This exercise was undertaken only to illustrate the nature of the problem. It is too crude to be a realistic guide. In any real population some grandparents would continue to live on their own even after the death of their spouse (this happened often in pre-industrial England). Some would remarry among the population of widows and widowers. Some might live with unmarried offspring; and so on. And in any case the figure of 29 per cent relates only to the class of households which contained parents and children. There were other households in all populations and their existence entails a lower overall percentage figure for three-generation households. Nevertheless even a crude exercise like this gives some perspective to the information which existed at the beginning – that 15 per cent of all households contained three generations. In the light of the findings from the model, and bearing in mind the various 'wastages' which must reduce the model figure of 29 per cent, it is clear that three-generation households were usual in the community in question (assuming, of course, that the model states its demography and pattern of social behaviour reasonably accurately).

Other examples of the importance of a knowledge of the properties of given combinations of fertility, mortality and nuptiality spring to mind. In some societies matrilineal cross-cousin marriages are regarded by the community as the best, to be concluded wherever possible. It is interesting in view of this to learn that the results obtained from computer simulation of a wide range of combinations of demographic variables suggests that it is impossible that in any historical society more than one tenth of all marriages can have been of this type.[34] Or again, it can be shown that if it is assumed that in general a man must wait to marry until his father dies and leaves him a holding, then if mortality rises generally a lowering in age of marriage results (because holdings become available earlier). This in turn increases fertility in a manner which over a wide range of possible mortality levels almost exactly counter-balances the increased mortality. The rate of growth or stability in number of the population is therefore unaffected by fluctuations in mortality in cases where this assumption is valid.[35]

The general picture

We have now briefly reviewed the ways in which fertility and mortality characteristics of pre-industrial populations may be said to have been under personal or social control. Inevitably with so vast a topic much has been left unsaid. For example, more might have been made of the very intricate interlinking between fertility and mortality – perhaps by showing how an increase in adult death rates, by decreasing the average length of unions could reduce fertility also; perhaps by examining the point that certain types of disease may have a considerable effect on fertility, some directly like syphilis, some indirectly by producing a marked disinclination for intercourse. But enough has been said to show in how many different ways a society might respond as its circumstances changed.

How did societies respond? It may be assumed to be true of all pre-industrial societies that at some point increasing numbers prejudice the living standards at least of the great bulk of the population living and labouring on the land. Living standards will then tend to fall unless the trend is reversed or advances occur in material culture sufficiently great to raise the optimum population size to a new and higher level.

One very simple model of relationships which has enjoyed a great vogue in many different guises is the view that a negative-feedback system will operate to prevent living standards from wandering very far from some existing level. It may be said, for example, that if wages rise men will be encouraged to marry earlier, and this in turn if there is little control of conception within marriage will tend to increase fertility. In as much as there is control of conception within marriage the motives for restriction are weakened if the married couples are blessed with greater affluence than usual. Malthus held to one version of this model. Hence his dislike of the Speenhamland system of poor relief which rescued labourers from their impetuosity in contracting marriages by guaranteeing to them and their families in times of high bread prices relief which was proportional to the size of the family. In his view this removed one of the strongest reasons for exercising restraint over the decision to marry. The 'passion between the sexes' was very powerful in any case. It was folly to do anything to undermine any bulwarks which helped to keep it in check. The operation of normal negative feedback was thus frustrated.

Logically a model of this type implies that if for any reason living standards fall there should either be a fall in fertility, or an increase in mortality, or both, so that numbers fall and the former balance is restored by homeostatic adjustment. But in the main those who think in terms of this model have tended to see a much greater ease of adjustment in one direction than in the other. It has been remarked, for example, that 'As soon as it becomes possible for a family to exist from the production of a smaller farm, the average size of farm goes down'[36] (and the population of course goes up). This assertion has been echoed many times, but its converse – that where, say, the productivity of the land has declined the average size of farm will immediately increase (and population fall) – is seldom voiced. The balance may be preserved, but if it is upset, the general expectation is that it will be upset in a damaging direction.

There is no lack of examples to support the somewhat gloomy view that the best that can be hoped for is that things will not get worse. One instance may serve here. The late seventeenth century in Belgian Flanders, as in much of western Europe, was a period in which population did not increase. Indeed in some areas it declined, following a period of population pressure in the first half of the century. The decline was quite marked in the parishes of Le Vieux-bourg, a poor, sandy area; much less marked and of shorter duration in the more fertile parishes of the Pays d'Alost. At the start of the eighteenth century there was a rough equality of births and deaths in both areas. Growth began again in the Pays d'Alost in the 1720s but only 20 years later in Le Vieuxbourg. Rates of growth in the Pays d'Alost were never high and may have declined in the second half of the century, and after some early growth in rural industry there was a return to agriculture in the later decades. The fertile soil lent itself to increasingly intensive farming and in the main the growth of population did no more than keep in step with the improvement of the soil's productivity. Population growth in this area did not get out of hand: the living standards of the population did not suffer and may even have improved towards the end of the century with the intensification of agriculture: a homeostatic balance of numbers in relation to their means of support was preserved.[37]

The course of events in Le Vieuxbourg, on the other hand, justifies the pessimistic view. Here growth began later but then gained momentum and by the end of the century the area was exhibiting the classic signs of overpopulation, with living standards miserably low for the bulk of the population. Since the density of population was already high and the soils poor agriculture could not absorb the rapidly growing labour force. As the century wore on more and more people turned to handicraft industry, and there was a rapid expansion in linen manufacture. The rural proletariat

Table 4·6 Fertility in Le Vieuxbourg and Pays d'Alost[38]
(ratio of births to marriages)

	Le Vieuxbourg	Pays d'Alost
1706—15	4·2	4·2
1716—25	4·3	4·3
1726—35	4·5	4·4
1736—45	4·7	4·8
1746—55	4·8	4·7
1756—65	5·0	4·7
1766—75	5·3	4·7
1776—85	5·0	4·4
1786—95	5·1	4·3

which resulted was often unable to obtain regular work. At harvest time when the demand for agricultural labour reached a peak they returned briefly to the land. In the rest of the year they depended on work put out to them by the linen manufacturers. Yet in Le Vieuxbourg fertility was higher than in Pays d'Alost, and whereas the ratio of births to marriages had begun to fall in the latter towards the end of the century, in the former it fell only slightly from the high level reached in the 1750s and 1760s.

In Le Vieuxbourg any pre-existing system of homeostatic adjustment keeping men and the means of livelihood in a constant relationship broke down badly in the later eighteenth century. And what happened in Le Vieuxbourg also happened many times elsewhere. The putting out system of rural industry gave to a surplus population only a slender means of support but they were in a poor bargaining position and any additional income was welcome. The result of this grasping at straws, however, was to aggravate the problem of population balance in the long run. If, for example, the effect of the possibility of earning a pittance from the domestic textile industry was to sidestep some of the old sanctions against early marriage (perhaps by destroying the old connection between marriage and a holding), it could clearly heighten the difficulty since it would tend to increase fertility and the rate of population growth. This tends towards the 'high pressure' equilibrium situation (see pages 48–9) with fertility and mortality both at high levels and standards of living low. Ultimately the area may be racked by a Malthusian spasm. In the case of the Flemish provinces the 1840s were a particularly miserable period though rather because of the impact of the industrial revolution than because of circumstances typical of pre-industrial society. The machine-spun thread of the Armentières factories across the French border and of the mills in England was cheaper than the thread from the local cottage industry. In the worst years population in the provinces as a whole declined and in some of the smaller units the fall was severe.[39]

The lurch into poverty brought about by rapidly increasing population is a good illustration of the closeness and complexity of the interaction between demographic, economic and social structural factors in history. The same position might be reached in many ways, having some features in common but also significant points of difference.

For example, it has been suggested that '. . . the single heir system tended to retard population growth and division to promote it'.[40] Where partible inheritance obtained, rural industry often grew up as the surplus labour searched for an economic niche on which to establish itself (in this system of inheritance all sons had a claim upon their father's property at his death).[41] Rural industry, poverty and population growth were closely associated. The initial impetus to industrial growth, however, might be quite different (the result, say, of a technique or resource peculiar to the area). Yet if, as a result, there was a breakdown in the pattern of behaviour developed by the community to keep its population size well adjusted to the local means of livelihood, the demographic results were much the same and 'high-pressure' problems loomed ahead. In either case the final position is damaging to the long terms prospects for economic growth because where wages are low primitive techniques tend to be the most profitable.[42] The feedback between demographic, social and economic conditions is sufficiently strong to make a state of stable misery all too likely.

The process of homeostatic adjustment of population numbers in societies whose material culture was both advanced and still developing appears to have been less simple and less sensitive than in some animal societies and in many primitive human societies where material culture was neither advanced nor changed rapidly (see pages 39–44). However, it would be dangerous to assume that populations in homeostatic balance are necessarily better situated than those which are not. It is possible that when numbers grow more rapidly than the flow of products from the agricultural base of the economy grave difficulties may arise and living standards become depressed. But it is also possible that the challenge may produce a new advance in material culture, allowing a larger population to be supported in equal or greater comfort. Again, it is possible that if population begins to expand rapidly this will raise aggregate demand sufficiently to encourage the development of larger production units, the introduction of better machines, and the improvement of methods of distribution which lower the cost of the product. In these circumstances a rapidly growing population introduces a greater dynamism into the economy and supports improvements in the techniques of producing wealth which allow both population and living standards to rise further. A population could, in short, move from worse to better as well as from better to worse. Lurches could occur in both directions as a result of insensitive adjustments between population variables and economic conditions.

Patterns of social behaviour and their associated demographic characteristics were often slow to change. The notion of leads and lags is helpful here, particularly for changes in age at marriage and fertility in general. A delayed response in, say, age at marriage to changing economic conditions might itself in turn provoke further economic changes, as well as being intimately bound up with other aspects of social behaviour. By introducing the idea of time lags into the model of relationships set out in figure 4·1, for example, some interesting further possibilities appear.

The history of Colyton's population provides a striking instance both of the absence of quick response in marriage habits to changing circumstances, and of the possibility of lurches in either direction which this implies. During most of the sixteenth century and the first few decades of the seventeenth population was rising rapidly in England, but thereafter for a further century it grew very little. Indeed in many places the earlier growth gave way to decline. During the period of rapid population growth real incomes fell. Prices rose tremendously in the sixteenth century but wages in general lagged well behind. When population growth had died away, however, real incomes stabilised and in many areas probably began to rise slowly in the later decades of the seventeenth and the early decades of the eighteenth century. Direct evidence about the course of real wages in Colyton is lacking but they are unlikely to have moved contrary to national trends over this long period.

If marriage decisions in Colyton had reflected sensitively the changes in real income, the average age at first marriage of women should have tended to rise during the sixteenth century as population pressure grew. After the middle of the seventeenth century the average age should have tended to fall again. In fact matters turned out quite differently, for over the long period from 1560 to the 1640s the average age at first marriage of both men and women did not change at all but thereafter rose sharply (see table 3·5) for women and slightly for men. Moreover, marital fertility was lower in this period than earlier and the two changes together produced much lower general fertility rates than before. It is hard to resist the conclusion that this phase of Colyton's demographic history represents a lurch in the opposite direction to that of Le Vieuxbourg a hundred years later. If economic growth was being prejudiced, it was certainly not by an excessive press of numbers: and if real incomes were rising (which is probable) the fertility schedule was notably slow to respond in a 'Malthusian' way.

During the eighteenth century the average age of women at first marriage in Colyton fell very slowly and fertility rates rose somewhat, which was perhaps the 'right' reaction to the changing economic environment. But in the early nineteenth century age at marriage fell and the fertility rates rose much more sharply – apparently the 'wrong' reaction at a time when real incomes were probably barely holding their own. Thus Colyton's history shows lurches in both directions. Each of the first two produced a compensatory movement in fertility after rather a long time lag – a homeostatic adjustment over the long term, so to say. The last change proved quite different. At any previous period such a sudden spurt of population growth would have meant a marked fall in real incomes and sooner or later would have led to a violent check to population growth (as happened in Ireland, of course). But this was the England of the industrial revolution, a period of change so fundamental that many of the expectations confirmed so often by painful experience in the past were to prove false for the new era. To this theme much of the next chapter is devoted.

Perhaps the most important lesson of this chapter (as of figure 4·1 at its beginning) should be that the interconnection between economic, social and demographic affairs is so intimate that but for the convenience of initial exposition there is little to be said for establishing in print clear cut divisions which hardly exist in the complexity of any given pre-industrial society. Relationships of cause and connections of function extend to and fro between elements in the complex in a bewildering way, so that clarity and comprehensiveness are in constant tension in any exposition of this sector of history. Certain themes may stand out: how important the combination of fertility and mortality rates was in

determining levels of real income; how wide were the ramifications
of different systems of inheritance; how the frequency, type and
severity of its demographic crises can reveal so much about a
society in the past; and so on. But different areas, periods and
social groups behaved very differently, and one of the fascinations
of this type of historical investigation lies in the precision with
which the nature of some of these differences may be laid bare.
Post-industrial societies are sometimes said to be 'converging'
towards a common demographic, economic and sociological
pattern.[43] If this is so, it follows not only that the present is
uniform but that the pre-industrial past was diverse.

5 Population and the industrial revolution

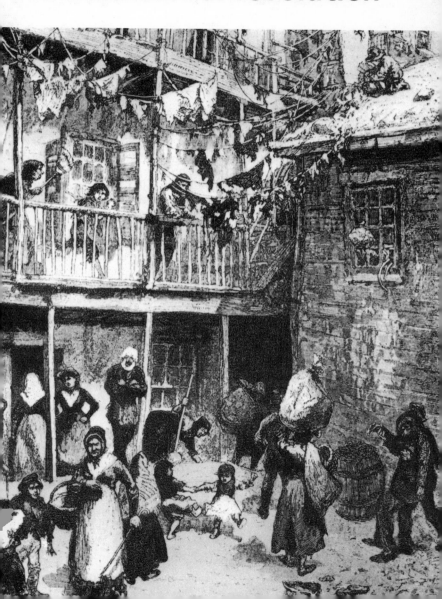

5 Population and the industrial revolution

The importance of the industrial revolution in demographic history can hardly be exaggerated. In its wake have come fundamental changes in demographic behaviour, in population distribution, in employment structure, in the relative size of urban and rural populations, and in the sources available for the study of population. So sweeping have these changes been that the old categories of analysis are sometimes inapplicable. The new wine is apt to burst the old bottles. Yet since all the major changes brought about by the industrial revolution have been mirrored in the changing demography of industrial societies, historical demography is a convenient mode of entry into the study of many aspects of that extraordinary set of related changes we call the industrial revolution.

Characteristics of the industrial revolution

We have seen that negative feedback between certain key economic and demographic variables was a distinguishing mark of all pre-industrial societies, which suffered by definition from an inability to engender a sustained growth in real incomes per head. It follows that during the industrial revolution the pattern of relationships changed with positive feedback replacing negative in some important sectors of the total network. As an illustration of a positive feedback situation within a sector of this network, consider the model in figure 5·1 showing the effect of the rapid growth of London upon English economy and society in the eighteenth century. The diagram also shows how close were the links between demographic, economic and sociological changes in this period.

Since all the relationships in the diagram are positive there is no point in labelling the connecting arrows with plus and minus signs as in figure 4·1. The sole distinction made is between those relationships which are reciprocal (shown with an arrow in each direction) and those where the relationship is one-way only. Thus the growth of London promoted improvements in transport media (for example it greatly stimulated the development of coastal shipping), and these improvements in turn facilitated its further growth.

Figure 5·1 The growth of London and the industrial revolution in England.

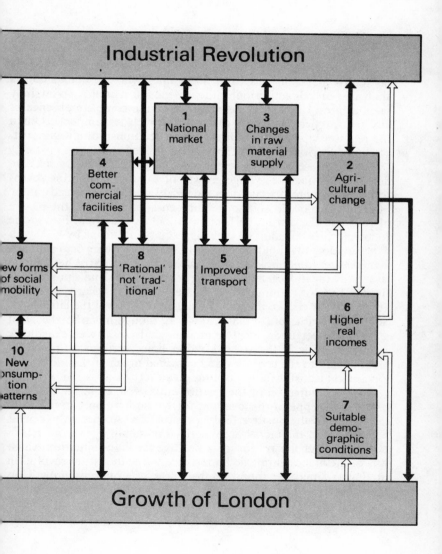

Hence the arrows leading to and from box 5. But though improved transport (box 5) stimulated agricultural change (box 2) by increasing the size of the market which each farmer could reach, there is no return arrow in this case. Sometimes where a connection is shown in one direction only, the absence of a return arrow may seem arbitrary. It is not meant to imply the complete absence of any return effect, but only that this is much less important than the relationship shown. Indirect return relationships always exist, of course, by longer paths through the model.

The model seeks to represent some of the results of a massive demographic fact – the huge growth of London during the seventeenth and eighteenth centuries. In 1650 London was already a city of about 350,000. In spite of the immense loss of life in the plague of 1665 and the disruption brought about by the Great Fire in the following year, London was the biggest city in Europe by 1700 with a population of about 550,000. By 1800 the figure had reached 900,000 and London was about twice the size of Paris, her nearest rival. Already in 1650 about seven per cent of England's population lived in London; a hundred years later 11 per cent (Paris contained about two per cent of the total French population at the later date). Some of the cities of the classical world, though much smaller, had a malign effect upon local economies and could with reason be termed parasitic. In the case of London, however, its growth brought great benefit to the economy and provided much of the impetus to the general transformation of English society.[1]

A full examination of the relationships depicted in the model is outside the scope of this chapter, for I wish here only to illustrate the nature of the positive feedback situation. Accordingly, only a few aspects of the model are described in detail.

An excellent illustration of a positive feedback situation which was of the highest strategic importance to the industrial revolution in England may be found in the effect of London's growth on English agriculture. As London grew it required larger and larger quantities of food. This produced revolutionary changes in agricultural practice, at first only within a limited radius of the city, but by the beginning of the eighteenth century over a large part of England. As more and more farmers became orientated to market demand in this way, traditional agricultural methods began to disappear, new crops were grown, the drift of land into enclosure was accentuated, and more food was produced more cheaply (and cheaper food meant higher real wages; hence the arrow to box 6). To ensure and expand supplies London merchants dealing in meat, fruit, poultry, and so on, took an increasing interest in the conditions of production and pumped capital and commercial expertise into the production units. The whole process greatly accelerated the transformation of English agriculture while at the same time assuring supplies of cheap food to London. Each step in the process helped to make the next step easier.

The group of three boxes to the left of the diagram (8, 9 and 10) cover closely related social changes. Breaking free from 'traditional' and adopting 'rational' attitudes and values means placing more emphasis on achievement than inherited position; ceasing to accept established modes of behaviour without inquiry simply because they have long existed; replacing custom by contract; and above all viewing economic affairs as the domain of calculation and flexible adjustment to changing circumstances rather than a proper sphere for the exercise of prescriptive rights and the fulfilment of customary obligations. It means the strengthening of new groups in society who do not subscribe to the values of the elites of traditional society. Ability is not recirculated through long-established social channels but can be absorbed into those groups whose activities cause society to change further. 'Rational' attitudes also lead to new habits of consumption with lower classes emulating their betters and no longer restricted by custom or sumptuary laws. The age of high mass consumption is just around the corner (and new wants create a new desire to work; hence the arrow from box 10 to box 6).

That the growth of London both facilitated and was facilitated by better commercial services, improved transport and the development of a general national market hardly needs underlining (boxes 1, 4 and 5). Nor will the relationships shown with box 3 (changes in raw material supply) cause surprise in view of what was written above (see pages 56–9). London's growth had a good deal to do with the development of coal mining in England (about a sixth of the whole coal output of the kingdom was shipped down the coast to London from the Tyne and Wear coal staithes in the eighteenth century and this kept busy half the nation's shipping). So much hinged upon the growth of the coal industry that this stimulus was important. Equally, without access to coal in quantity as a substitute for wood both the domestic hearths and many of the industries of the capital would have been put to greater expense and might not have been able to continue to maintain themselves at all.

Finally box 7, suitable demographic conditions, connotes a situation in which population does not expand so rapidly when real incomes are rising that the upward trend is quickly reversed – a negative feedback situation typical of many pre-industrial societies. This may come about because fertility is low and numbers rise little or not at all when real incomes move upwards, but it can also be the result of the existence of areas of exceptionally high death rates and a burial surplus serving to counterbalance other areas where there are more births than deaths. London was a most unhealthy city in the early eighteenth century when a net immigration of perhaps 8,000–10,000 a year was needed to make good the burial surplus and allow the city to continue to grow. Its continued growth acted as a brake upon the growth of English population *in toto* and so helped to avoid the occurrence of a 'Malthusian' cycle of events. Box 7 like box 10 is, therefore, connected to box 6 (higher real wages) in the model.

All the developments shown in the numbered boxes helped either directly or indirectly to produce the industrial revolution in England (indeed they *were* a large part of the industrial revolution) and were further advanced as the industrial revolution progressed. Hence the further sets of arrows connecting the numbered boxes with the large box at the top of the diagram. The model covers, of course, only a fraction of the total complex of changes going forward at the time.

In other sectors of the total phenomenon there were much weightier obstacles to overcome (or, to phrase it differently, negative feedback was more in evidence).

Though London's role in promoting the industrial revolution was both interesting and important, this was not the main reason for including the model shown in figure 5·1 in this chapter. It was introduced because it provides one example of a set of relationships which may help a society to escape from the characteristic limitations of pre-industrial life, and because it illustrates very well the typically close connections between demographic, sociological and economic elements in the process of change. But though this may help to make clear what the industrial revolution was, it tells little of the characteristic demographic changes which took place in the countries caught up in the industrial revolution, and to these changes and their effects we now turn.

Population changes in England

From time to time attempts hve been made to assess the importance of English population history to the industrial revolution in that country, an event which preserves a special interest since it occurred first there. It has been argued on occasion, for example, that the rise in population which is noticeable after about 1750 in England was produced by the economic changes of the early stages of the industrial revolution. It has also been argued that the rise began before the industrial revolution was under way. One school of thought has it that because population growth was comparatively sluggish until late in the day, there was a severe shortage of labour which served as a stimulus to the development of machinery to carry out operations previously done by hand. Another has it that the press of population was a main cause of the rising home demand of the period and that this, by encouraging the economies of scale, played a large part in stimulating economic growth.

If one thing is clear about the fascinating tangle of relationships between population and economic and social change during the

English industrial revolution, it is that any simple concept of these relationships is impossible to sustain. Their characteristic complexity becomes evident if the history of other countries at this period is borne in mind and the diversity of experience in England itself is remembered. Two considerations may serve to illustrate this point.

First, economic historians have too easily assumed that there was something exceptional about the rate of growth of population in England in the eighteenth century. It is implicit in much that has been written on this subject that the very slow growth of population in England in the first half of the eighteenth century was normal for Europe at that time and that the acceleration which took place during the second half of the century was not paralleled elsewhere. Table 5·1 shows how inaccurate such an assumption is. In a number of European countries population growth in the eighteenth century was very swift by the general standards of pre-industrial societies, and was often at its swiftest in areas most remote from rapid economic change. Rates of growth as high as those in England occurred in many parts of Europe, and in many countries there was an acceleration of the rate of growth about the middle of the century. Comparison with table 5·12 shows that rates of growth did not in general change very much in the nineteenth century, contrary to what is often assumed. England, however, did break clear of the pack for a time during the first half of the nineteenth century, the period when the full impact of industrial revolution was being felt in England but before it affected most other countries to a comparable degree. One or two of the figures in table 5·1 may be open to correction. In particular the rate of growth of population in Hungary in the period 1754–89 is suspiciously high, but the close similarity between England and continental trends in the eighteenth century is hard to doubt in the light of this table.

The rapid growth of population in rural areas of traditional agriculture continued well into the nineteenth century. From 1816 to 1849 the population of Pomerania, for example, increased more rapidly than the combined total of Arnsberg and Düsseldorf (which

Table 5·1 Population growth in eighteenth century Europe (in '000s)[2]

	England & Wales	France	Italy	Sweden	Württemberg	East Prussia
1700	5,826 [a]	19,000	11,500		340	400
1720				1,450		
1740		20,000			472	
1750	6,140 [b]			1,740 [e]		
1800	9,156 [c]	25,000 [d]	18,000	2,347	660	931

	Pomerania	Silesia	Austria	Bohemia	Hungary
1700	120	1,000			
1720					
1740	309	1,100			
1750			1,360 [g]	1,940 [g]	3,000 [g]
1800	500	2,000 [f]	1,888 [d]	2,922 [d]	8,500 [d]

a 1701;   b 1751;   c 1801;   d 1789;   e 1749;   f 1804;   g 1754.

Percentage rates of growth per annum

England & Wales	1701–1801 = 0·45	East Prussia	1700–1800 = 0·84
	1751–1801 = 0·80	Pomerania	1740–1800 = 0·80
France	1700–89 = 0·31		
	1740–89 = 0·45	Silesia	1740–1804 = 0·94
Italy	1700–1800 = 0·45	Austria	1754–89 = 0·94
Sweden	1749–1800 = 0·59	Bohemia	1754–89 = 1·18
Württemberg	1740–1800 = 0·56	Hungary	1754–89 = 3·01

included the Ruhr), as table 5·2 shows. Only in the last period shown in the table, 1849–55, when industrial growth in and near the Ruhr coalfield began to get into its stride did the pace of growth in the more economically diversified area in the west begin to draw ahead of the purely agricultural east. Between 1816 and 1849 population increased 75 per cent in the eastern area compared with only 54 per cent in the western. Without the safety valve afforded by movement internally to the great administrative and trading cities and to the Ruhr coalfield, and externally to areas of European settlement in North and South America and Australia the population problems of those parts of Germany in which rural population multiplied so rapidly during the eighteenth and nineteenth centuries would have been serious indeed and an adjustment of Irish severity might have proved unavoidable (see map on page 157).

Nor was eastern Germany an exception to the normal pattern. Other parts of Europe in which there was no modern industry also experienced a rate of population growth which could reasonably be described as hectic by any earlier standards. In Norway, for example, the rate of increase rose to a peak early in the century which was largely sustained thereafter. The nineteenth-century rates were about twice those prevailing in the eighteenth century, itself a time of rapid growth. Not until the 1860s was there any large shift away from the traditional employment structure in Norway, and even though there were important advances in the productivity of the land within the traditional framework (notably by the introduction of the potato), here too a crisis could not have been long delayed but for the rapid growth in the timber industry in Norway itself and the large exodus of Norwegians to the United States.

A second consideration which helps to underline the diversity of demographic changes at the time of the industrial revolution is in a sense an extension of the first. It is essential to recognise that during the early decades of the industrial revolution in England and in other countries, the economic changes were local or at most regional phenomena. Employment structures and habits of life were revolutionised only in small areas at first. In time whole countries

Table 5·2 Population growth in two German areas in the first half of the nineteenth century (populations in '000s: percentage rates of growth per annum)[3]

	Prov. Pomerania		Reg.-Bez. Arnsberg and Düsseldorf	
Year	Population	Percentage	Population	Percentage
1816	683		968	
1822	801	2·69	1,037	1·16
1831	912	1·45	1,173	1·38
1840	1,056	1·64	1,340	1·49
1849	1,198	1·41	1,489	1·18
1855	1,289	1·23	1,639	1·61

Table 5·3 Population growth in Norway 1735–1865 (population in '000s; percentage rates of growth per annum)[4]

Year	Population	Percentage	Year	Population	Percentage
1735	616		1805	893	0·58
1745	622	0·09	1815	905	0·13
1755	671	0·76	1825	1,042	1·41
1765	720	0·71	1835	1,187	1·31
1775	741	0·29	1845	1,319	1·06
1785	790	0·64	1855	1,480	1·16
1795	843	0·65	1865	1,702	1·40

were caught up in the process but the leaven took several decades to affect the whole loaf. Local demographic changes were often the results of purely local situations. To deal with national aggregates can then be highly misleading. The chronology of change was local, too. The onset of rapid change varied considerably from area to area in demographic history just as in the history of industrial change, and developments big enough in scale to affect national aggregates occurred much later than the first local changes.

At the local scale of analysis, however, simple relationships between economic and demographic changes are no more easy to find. It may be plausible to attribute the sudden alteration in the balance of baptism and burial in, say, Worcestershire or Lancashire to the changes in train in the local economies. It is more difficult to do so in a parish like Hartland where the change was also marked and began about 1750, as early as in many industrial areas. Hartland was far from the small centres of new industrial growth. Its economic base did not begin to change for many years after the sudden appearance of substantial baptism surpluses. Nor was there any revolutionary change in transport facilities in the area such as might be adduced to explain the action at a distance of the new forces of industrial growth. Yet there were many parishes like Hartland and this fact in turn makes it less easy to accept the view that nascent industrial growth provoked the population changes even in areas close to the new centres of industry. More must be known of the changes in fertility and mortality themselves before we attempt to assimilate them into models of population change during the industrial revolution.

The demand for labour and demographic change

But before turning to a more detailed description of the changes in mortality and fertility which took place during and immediately after the industrial revolution, it may be useful to pursue a little further the investigation of a pattern often said to exist and to be of importance in explaining accelerated population growth – the view

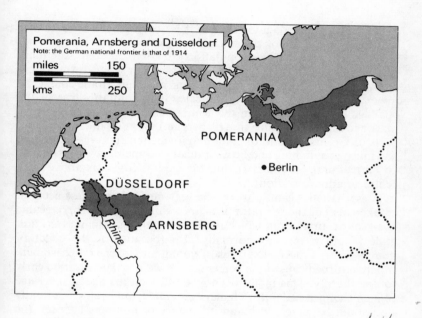

1 theory

that with economic growth the demand for labour also grew; and
that this caused an increase in fertility and so produced the additional labour needed (demand producing its required supply).
Several mechanisms have been suggested in this connection, but all
turn out to be fraught with difficulties of interpretation.

In as much as the new demand was for adult male labour and
was reflected in a rise in the wages offered to workers in the new
industrial areas, it might be expected that this would tend to lower
the age at which men married. The time lag between one generation
and the next is too great, of course, for an increased demand for
hands to be met efficiently in the short term by an increase in
fertility. The new-born child must wait almost two decades before
he can join the adult labour force. But a significant lowering in the

average age of marriage of men, if it is accompanied by a similar reduction in the age of their brides will, other things being equal, increase fertility and cause population growth to quicken. And there is evidence that the average age at marriage for women was low in areas where the demand for male labour was high. In the coalfields, for example, this was usually the case. It was notably true of the coalfield industrial areas in the Ruhr. Table 5·4 shows how early marriage came for women in Arnsberg in 1880 compared with other parts of Germany with different employment structures (Arnsberg had much coal mining and heavy industry; Pomerania was primarily an agricultural province; Berlin, the capital city, was above all a centre of administration).

These statistics can, however, be very misleading unless account is taken also of the sex ratio of men to women in the marriageable age-groups. In areas in which there was a strong demand for adult male labour there was normally also (because of the effect of immigration) a marked surplus of young men over young women, which in turned caused the percentage of women who married early to rise sharply. This might occur even though the age at marriage of men changed little. Both female general fertility rates and family size would be increased by an imbalance of numbers between the sexes of this sort without necessarily proving that the effect had been quite what appears at first sight. If the increased early marriage among women in these areas were counterbalanced by a decreased likelihood of marriage for women in the areas from which the male immigrants came (because the sex balance here was upset in the opposite direction), then the total effect of the changes upon the fertility of the population as a whole would be slight, and might be negative rather than positive. The whole argument from levels of wages to early marriage is too crude to be acceptable unless it is considerably amplified. It was the total environment in which men and women lived rather than the simple level of wages, or even a combination of wage level and employment expectation, which influenced decisions to marry. It is noticeable, for example, that both in France and Germany marital and general fertility rates

Table 5·4 Proportions of women ever married in Germany in 1880 (per 1,000 total female population)[5]

| | Age-groups | | | | | |
	15–19	20–4	25–9	30–4	35–9	40–4
Arnsberg	22	373	781	900	922	924
Pomerania	15	258	643	822	*879	904
Berlin	16	224	571	765	836	862

Table 5·5 General and marital fertility rates in France and Prussia about 1880[6]

| | France (1880–2) | | | Prussia (1879–81) | | |
		General fertility	Marital fertility		General fertility	Marital fertility
Industrial areas	Nord	147	280	Arnsberg	204	351
				Düsseldorf	181	358
Great Cities	Seine	99	150	Berlin	138	255
				Hamburg	146	271
	France	**112**	**196**	**Prussia**	**168**	**314**

Note
General fertility: total children born per annum per 1,000 women 15–44.
Marital fertility: total legitimate children born per annum per 1,000 married women 15–44.

were rather low in the large administrative and trading cities in the nineteenth century, though rather high in the industrial areas; yet it would be difficult to maintain that in the one type of area incomes were much below and in the other much above the national averages.

The argument from the demand for adult male labour does not stem simply from a change in wage rates, of course. It usually includes the further point that many men in the new industrial areas escaped altogether from the restrictions of the traditional apprenticeship system which had frequently delayed marriage in the past. Nor had they to wait to succeed to land before marrying. Moreover, in many new occupations (for example, coal mining) a man reached his maximum earning power when in his physical prime. Once he had attained this he could have no further motive for postponing marriage.

No doubt there is weight in these further considerations and they may conjointly explain some changes in marriage habits and fertility during the industrial revolution. But once more German demographic history in the nineteenth century shows the danger of generalisation. Table 5·6 shows that in 1880 there were more men married in the early age groups in East Prussia, remote, rural and far from prosperous, than in the wealthier agricultural areas further west like Hannover or Münster, or even than in the new industrial areas like Düsseldorf, Arnsberg or Aachen (the province and the *Regierungs-bezirk* are rather clumsy measures to use because they are not 'pure' in occupational structure but this only dampens out differences without obscuring them altogether). This may have been due in part, once again, to the sex ratio since there was a very large surplus of women in East Prussia, but the point is suggestive nonetheless, especially as age at marriage of men is usually less influenced by the sex ratio than that of women. In Germany at this time there seems good reason to believe that the most important single factor affecting age at marriage was religious adherence. Protestant areas on the whole married early (East Prussia, Hannover and to a lesser degree Minden and Arnsberg); Catholic areas late (Münster, Aachen and to a lesser degree Düsseldorf). It is of course true that

Table 5·6 Proportions of men ever married in Germany in 1880 (per 1,000 total male population)[7]

| | Age-groups | | | | | |
	15–19	20–24	25–29	30–34	35–39	40–44
East Prussia	2	97	529	817	894	919
Hannover	2	73	439	733	850	894
Minden	2	85	487	770	874	903
Arnsberg	1	91	486	763	861	893
Münster	1	42	302	608	765	824
Düsseldorf	2	82	452	736	831	867
Aachen	1	43	315	610	741	796

even in areas where the overall marriage pattern seems to have been relatively little influenced by the demand for labour and wage levels, economic fluctuations had a great effect on short-term changes. There was, for example, a clear-cut tendency for marriage rates in the short term to vary inversely with the price of bread.

An alternative link has sometimes been suggested between industrial growth and high fertility. Where there was a large demand for child labour, it has at times been claimed that this increased fertility because it gave parents a strong incentive to have large families. This assertion is not necessarily connected with changes in age at marriage, but may refer simply to a fall in the average interval between births which might raise fertility considerably quite independently of any changes in age at marriage. The argument runs that when children were able to gain paid employment at a very

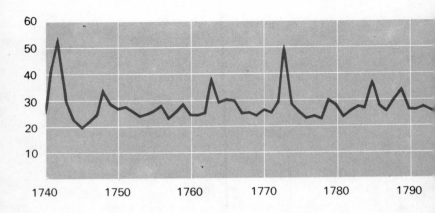

Figure 5·2 The Norwegian crude death rate 1740–1850 (per 1000 total population).[8]

early age (in England in the early nineteenth century the cotton mills often employed children at the age of eight or nine, and even occasionally five or six) parents could expect them to add to the household income after only a few dependent years. The argument implies that this had not previously been the case. It also implies that the income to parents from children who were out at work more than counterbalanced the continued expenditure on them for food and clothing, or at least that parents believed that these things were so.

Both these assumptions require more buttressing than they have received in the past. In pre-industrial times a child might also be of economic benefit to the household as a whole even though he might receive no cash payment for it. Either the father engaged upon the land, or the mother sitting at a domestic craft might be helped by their children from a young age, and the total income of the household would in that case increase, in some cases no doubt as substantially as from the wages of children working in factories or mines. Children's wages in these places of work were naturally only a fraction of an adult's wage, especially in their youngest years. It might well not be until a child was in his teens that he earned

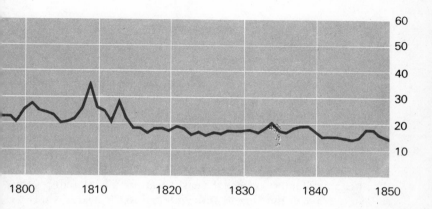

much more than his maintenance cost his parents. Before then he would continue to be a net liability.[9] It must not be overlooked that large families not only meant higher family expenditure week by week but also higher outlay on the house itself and its equipment (unless a cut in living standards is admitted which undermines the argument from large families to greater prosperity). Ten children require more beds and bedding, more cutlery and plates, more chairs, larger cooking pots, and even simply a larger house than five children if living standards are to be maintained. And some at least of these expenditures are incurred before their earning power has begun, certainly before it is more than trivial.

Where there is clear evidence that the mean birth interval did fall significantly among a population in an industrialising area three further points should be borne in mind. The first has been made in a different connection already. It is dangerous to attach special significance to changes in an industrial area if similar changes were taking place also in other types of area at much the same time. Mean birth intervals, for example, were falling quite steeply at Colyton in the late eighteenth and early nineteenth centuries though Colyton was far from any of the seats of the English industrial revolution. Secondly, the possibility that changes of habit brought about by industrialisation may have had a direct effect on birth intervals should not be overlooked. For example, it is conceivable that the normal length of suckling period may have been shorter than in the countryside. This would probably hold true of married women who did work, full or part time (in domestic service as well as in factories) outside the home. Early weaning would tend to reduce the intergenesic interval. The third point is related to the second. There is some evidence that infant mortality increased in the industrialising districts. In the worst of these areas it reached very high levels. In as much as this was so it would tend to reduce the intergenesic interval since the early death of a baby reduces (by, say, an average of nine months) the interval to the next birth. If we imagine, for the sake of argument, a population in which the over-crowded living conditions of a spreading industrial slum increased the risk of infection for small babies enough to drive up infant mortality from 150 to 250 per 1,000 live births, then, without any change in 'real' fertility, the mean interval between births would fall somewhat. In this instance if the mean normal interval between births were 30 months and the mean interval after an early death in the first year of life were 21 months, then the rise in infant mortality would cause a fall in the mean overall birth interval from 28·7 to 27·8 months. A major shortening of the average suckling period might have a considerably greater effect.

Since it is evident that no simple general model of the relationship between demographic changes and the industrial revolution is likely to 'save the phenomena', it will prove useful to examine the changes of mortality and fertility which occurred and so discover how far generalisation can be taken.

Mortality

It is convenient and logical to begin an account of the long term population changes brought about by the industrial revolution with mortality. The fall in mortality usually preceded the equally fundamental changes in fertility, and fertility changes are best understood against the background of falling death rates. Several features of the revolutionary changes which occurred deserve to be stressed.

The first is the almost complete elimination of crises of the old type, whether brought about by harvest failure or by the independent operation of epidemic disease. There were inevitably some exceptions to this rule, such as the great cholera outbreaks, or, perhaps the most dramatic of all, the great Irish famine which began in 1845, a disaster whose extent was curiously underlined by the fact that Ireland's nearest neighbour England led the van of the industrial revolution (the population of Ireland was 8,200,000 in 1841 but when the next census was taken in 1851 it was only 6,514,000, a fall of just over 20 per cent from death and emigration). Much more typical, however, was the course of events in Norway. In that country from 1815 onwards the old fluctuations in the crude death rate largely disappeared. Years like 1742, 1773 and 1809 no longer recurred. As figure 5·2 shows the new plateau-like mortality curve was not substantially lower than the level of the death rate in the eighteenth century outside the years of poor harvest and disease, but now the low level was consistently held and tended to drift down, whereas previously the curve was much less smooth. It was a characteristic of death rates of pre-industrial European societies in general that in most years they were appreciably lower than birth rates, so that outside the periodic crisis years population grew fairly quickly, typically perhaps by from five to ten per 1,000 per annum. In most countries, as in Norway, the disappearance of pre-industrial demographic conditions was signalled by the elimination of the sudden surges of mortality which had kept population totals within bounds in earlier centuries. The timing of the disappearance of the old pattern varied considerably from country to country. In most parts of France, for example, it was fading fast by the middle of the eighteenth century.

The reasons for the dying away of the old switchback motion are many. Bad harvests are much less likely to produce severe deprivation

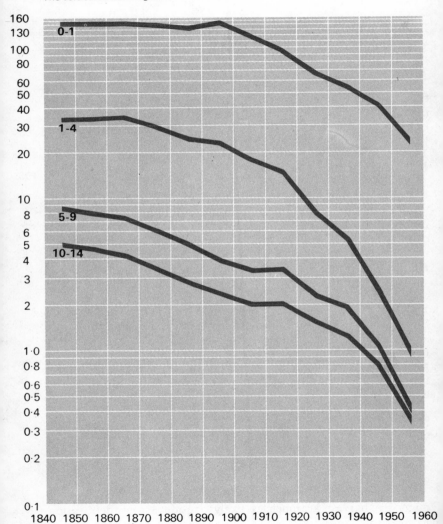

Figure 5·3 Age-specific death rates in England and Wales 1840–1960 (per 1000 living; for infant mortality per 1000 live births). The rates for the age group 1–4 are approximations until the figure for 1931–40.[10] The vertical scale is logarithmic.

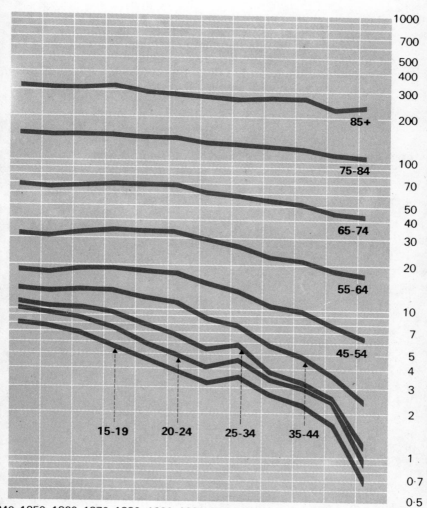

when communications are good than when each small area depends largely upon its own resources. This was shown with special clarity in India when the main trunk railway system was built. Although there was no great revolution in the productivity of Indian agriculture at that time the railways made it possible to balance out harvest surpluses in one region against harvest deficits elsewhere much more effectively, and if necessary to distribute grain imported from abroad. The levelling out of European death rates occurred before the advent of the railways but the last decades of the eighteenth century and the first of the nineteenth saw a notable easing of transport problems with the improvement of roads, the construction of canals, the development of river navigation and a great increase in ocean-going shipping. In addition the man-made obstacles to internal transport, river dues, dues to be paid on entry to cities, dues at the movement from one petty kingdom to another, disappeared in the wake of French revolutionary armies or were much reduced by administrative reform.

In some areas there was an important broadening of the food base of the local population with the addition of the potato to the staple foods available. In areas where the potato grows freely it produces far more food to the acre than alternative cereal crops. It can also be grown, particularly on the wetter and cooler margins of the continent, in areas in which other food crops do not grow well and stand in danger of failing to ripen at all in many years. In such areas the acceptance of the potato as a main food crop brought a new dependability in the supply of food. Years which were unfavourable to cereal culture might leave the potato un-affected. The conspicuous damping down in the fluctuations of the deaths in Norway after 1815 was probably due in part to this. In many other areas too – Ireland, Germany, Poland, and so on, the potato rapidly became a staple food. And there were other changes in agricultural practice which were also very helpful in increasing the reliability of the food supply and improving the quality of diet. The introduction of roots and clovers enabled larger numbers of livestock to be maintained and kept through the winter. The elimination of fallow years by suitable rotation of crops combined with the use of more animal manure gave a double boost to agricultural productivity since not only did it add considerably to the acreage which could be cultivated in any one year, but it benefited the soil as well so that yields per acre increased. Better drainage, better breeds of sheep and cattle, new types of agricultural machinery (notably seed drills), better storage facilities, and so on, all helped, though there were wide regional variations in the speed of adoption of better practices.

A second feature common to the mortality history of most of western Europe lies in the changes in age-specific death rates which took place. In all the major western countries which were caught up by the industrial revolution expectation of life at birth improved, slowly at first but with increasing rapidity towards the end of the nineteenth century. In general death rates fell much more among children and teenagers than among adults. The proportional fall in death rates tended to decline steadily with age until in middle life and later there was little difference between the levels obtaining at the beginning and the end of the nineteenth century as figure 5·3 shows. There was, however, one major exception to the rule that the biggest falls in death rates were in the younger age-groups. The youngest of all the age-groups conventionally used by demographers is the age-group 0–1. Infant mortality showed no tendency to fall in most parts of western Europe until the last years of the century. Before then the figures often tended to rise rather than fall. In part this may be due to improvements in registration. Infant deaths are more likely than any others to escape registration during the early years of a vital statistics service. This introduces some uncertainty into the interpretation of the figures, and here, as for so many other topics, more local, detailed studies are needed to provide a surer foundation of knowledge, but the contrast between the movements of infant and general child mortality provides an interesting clue to the nature of the mortality changes of the nineteenth century as a whole.

During the period of heaviest infant mortality in the first days and weeks of life a baby is dependent on his mother for food, so that the type and quantity of his food does not alter much over a wide range of environmental conditions. Children at this age, are, however, highly susceptible to infectious diseases of the stomach and chest. A radical improvement in infant mortality, therefore, is only likely when the nature of these infections is understood and effective countermeasures are available. Only at the end of the nineteenth century was the necessary knowledge attained. Thereafter the improvement was rapid and great. Infant mortality rates have fallen by a factor of five or more since the beginning of the twentieth century. The earlier improvements in diet and public sanitation, however, (for example a purer water supply) had little effect on infant mortality, while the crowded conditions of urban life tended to increase the risk of early infection.

Once a child had been weaned, however, matters were different. Infectious diseases were still the chief killers – cholera, typhus, tuberculosis, scarlet fever, whooping cough, rheumatic fever, smallpox, diphtheria, and so on – but now the quality and quantity of food available might make a marked difference both to susceptibility to disease and to the success with which the victim struggled with a disease once infected. Those who live in warm, dry houses and are well fed are far less likely to succumb to tuberculosis than those who do not. The medical history of the two world wars of this century has shown how quickly this and other infectious diseases can re-establish a hold upon populations if food is scarce and it is difficult to stay warm, dry and clean. The steady decline in the mortality rates of children and young adults during the nineteenth century in western Europe is testimony to the steady improvement in the environment in which young people lived.

The changes in mortality rates were not, by the standards of the developing world today, very swift or spectacular. They reflected the steady spread of many improvements in private and public hygiene and in the range and quality of foods which could be afforded. Cheaper soap could be bought with which both the person and the new and cheaper cotton clothing could be washed. Purer

Table 5·7 Expectation of life at birth in western countries in the nineteenth century (in years)[11]

Year	Male	Female		Year	Male	Female
1840	39·6	42·5		1880	43·9	46·5
1850	40·3	42·8		1890	45·8	48·5
1860	41·1	43·4		1900	48·9	52·1
1870	42·3	44·7		1910	52·7	56·0

Note average of Denmark, England and Wales, France, Massachusetts, Netherlands, Norway and Sweden.

Table 5·8 Infant mortality in France and Prussia (per 1,000 live-born)[12]

France	male	female		Prussia	male	female
1860–2	182	154		1860–2	213	184
1880–2	184	155		1879–81	218	188
1900–2	159	132		1899–1901	222	189
				1909–11	181	154

water was piped to the big cities, often from distant reservoirs, and, after the connection between sewage disposal, untreated water and the great cholera outbreaks of the mid-century had been established, the provision of sewerage systems was pursued as a matter of urgency and the chemical purification of water supplies began. Cheap supplies of coal made for better heating in winter even though air pollution increased. House construction improved especially after governments began to lay down minimum standards (in England the Artisans' Dwellings Act of 1875 was a milestone: Joseph Chamberlain cleared fifty acres of slums in Birmingham during the year after it became law).[13] Government action in other spheres was also cumulatively important; for example in founding systems of local medical officers of health and in legislation against the sale of adulterated food. Most important of all rising real incomes allowed people to buy more and better food and to resort less frequently to dangerous half-rotten grain and other substitutes for sound food. Standards of nutrition improved. At the end of the century the development of cheap fats using vegetable oils and the import of citrus fruits broadened still further the range of foodstuffs eaten by a larger and larger proportion of the population.

A third general feature of the industrial revolution period is the great variation in mortality found in different social and economic environments. The labours of men like Charles Booth and Rowntree in England and Frédéric Le Play in France, by painstaking investigation of the condition of individual families showed how ill many still lived even in the second half of the century. Undernourishment and deficiency diseases were still widely found. Rickets continued to deform legs and pelvises in industrial Lancashire throughout the century. Four men in every ten volunteering to serve in the British army in the Boer War were found unfit to bear arms.[14] Rowntree's work at York showed that ten per cent of the population even in 1899 lived in primary poverty, being unable to afford sufficient food to keep their calorie intake at the level he regarded as the absolute minimum for healthy existence even if they had used every penny in the most intelligent and economical manner possible. A further

18 per cent lived in secondary poverty in conditions often equally wretched. Even in 1898 infant mortality in the poorest areas at 247 per 1,000 live births was two-and-a-half times the level among those wealthy enough to employ servants (94 per 1,000).[15] Nor was York worse than other English towns. Neither Dickens nor Zola had to invent any of the horrors they portrayed. In England successive Royal or Parliamentary Commissions were able to produce a massive documentation at intervals during the century of the crudity, squalor and danger of the life of the industrial working classes. Engels never lacked harrowing illustrations of the thesis that the proletariat must become increasingly impoverished as the capitalist system ground towards its inevitable breakdown. And yet expectation of life, often a sensitive guide to conditions of life, increased without serious interruption in most countries for the greater part of the century.

It is of course incontestably true that mortality in the new industrial slums reached appalling levels. Expectation of life was very low indeed. In the mid-nineteenth century it was only 24·2 years for men in Manchester according to the calculations of William Farr, at a time when it was 40·2 years in England as a whole, and already 51·0 in Surrey, a state of affairs which Farr described as 'unnatural and susceptible of remedy'.[16] In the worst parts of cities like Liverpool and Manchester expectation of life was well under 20 years. In Glasgow the crude death rate was two-and-a-half times as high for families living in one or two rooms as for those in five or more rooms. In a study of urban life in late nineteenth-century Europe Adna Ferrin Weber quoted some very grim statistics of life in the Berlin of 1885, when an inquiry showed that half of all the deaths in the city occurred among the six per cent of the population living in families having only one room at their disposal.[17] The literature of all the industrialising countries of western Europe is full of novels examining the depths of misery into which people sank in the worst of the new slums and the immense toll of life exacted at all ages. Yet it would be as dangerous to base an assessment of the effect of the industrial revolution upon mortality on these facts and impressions as it would be to assume that the conditions which occurred in pre-industrial Europe during the periodic demographic crises were typical of pre-industrial times generally, for what was then concentrated into certain short periods of time was later concentrated into certain restricted areas.

During and after the industrial revolution the amplitude of fluctuation in death rates from year to year shrank, but the spread of rates between areas of different economic and social type probably did not. It may have even increased. How the impact of the industrial revolution upon mortality is viewed, therefore, will depend very largely upon the way in which the area of study is delimited. The slums of the old quarters of Lille contained some of the worst and deadliest living conditions in France during the period when the textile industry of Nord was in full expansion, but table 5·9 shows that expectation of life in the department as a whole was scarcely inferior to that found in Aisne and Somme, agricultural departments nearby which might have been expected to be substantially healthier, and was very close to the national figure. The remote but depressed Breton department, Finisterre, though entirely rural, was notably less healthy. Nord contained Lille itself, the textile complex of Roubaix-Tourcoing, the linen manufacturing centre of Armentières, the coal mines and iron works near Valenciennes. This is a fair cross-section of the early industrial revolution in occupational structure, and it would be difficult to argue that the area which Zola depicted in *Germinal* was notably healthy among industrial areas as a whole – and yet the total effect on expectation of life for the department as a whole was very slight.

It is perhaps more accurate to say that high mortality was caused by urbanisation rather than by industrialisation. It was in the bigger cities that mortality was so very high. Many of these big cities were not heavily engaged in the new industries but were administrative and commercial centres. Paris, Berlin, Marseilles, and Liverpool all had high death rates and low expectations of life, though none was a typical product of the industrial revolution in the narrow sense. In a broader sense, of course, all were able to develop only because

Table 5·9 Expectation of life at birth in France in the later nineteenth century (in years)[18]

| | Nord | | Aisne | |
	male	female	male	female
1861	40·8	41·1	41·6	44·6
1881	41·1	43·0	42·6	47·5
1901	44·6	48·1	46·6	50·8

| | Somme | | Finisterre | | FRANCE | |
	male	female	male	female	male	female
1861	41·1	43·1	35·4	37·3	40·1	41·3
1881	10·5	44·1	28·5	30·8	41·5	43·9
1901	45·2	49·3	42·5	45·6	45·4	48·9

of the improvements in transport and growth in productive capacity which characterise industrial revolution. To a notable extent, but now in a different context, mortality was still density-dependent. Wherever there were large cities there were slum areas with very high densities of population and severe overcrowding which allowed diseases like tuberculosis to spread very widely and exposed children and young people to a great range of infectious illness.

In the more strictly industrial areas, although very large populations in aggregate grew up round the pitheads, the factories, the mills and the furnaces, many people lived in comparatively small industrial villages and towns. The mortality experience of these areas was often suprisingly good. Table 5·10 shows the crude death

Table 5·10 Crude death and birth rates per 1,000 total population in the Ruhr, 1894—6 (birth rates in brackets)[19]

	Arnsberg	Düsseldorf	Aachen	Münster
Industrial Kreise	20·6(44·4)	20·3(40·2)	22·2(38·3)	22·1(51·3)
Other Kreise	19·6(35·5)	20·6(34·8)	21·8(32·9)	21·7(34·7)

rates in the main administrative divisions of the Ruhr in the middle 1890s. The differences between the industrial areas and the rest were very small. The age structure of the population in the industrial areas may in general have favoured them, but on the other hand birth rates in these *Kreise* were much higher and infantile deaths were a high proportion of the total which counts in the opposite sense. There is no reason to suppose that more refined measures of mortality would reveal a lower expectation of life in the industrial areas at this period.

Recent experience has shown that tremendous improvements in expectation of life and mortality at all except the highest ages can be achieved without any drastic change in the economic fortunes of society, when the techniques of modern public health and medicine are available. Expectation of life in Ceylon increased by almost ten years (from 42·2 to 51·8 years) in one year 1946—7,[20] about as much as in Europe in the whole of the nineteenth century, because of the virtual eradication of malaria and the progress made in combating other common diseases with modern drugs. In Europe it was not until the last years of the nineteenth century that the medical contribution to the reduction in mortality became clearly important. At that time a much fuller understanding of the nature and means of transmission of infectious diseases was achieved. With this came the possibility of developing effective drugs, vaccines and other therapeutic and preventive measures. A little earlier the appreciation of the importance of antiseptic measures in hospitals, the development of anaesthetics and improvements in surgical techniques themselves cut case mortalities for many conditions drastically. For the first time it became perfectly clear that the cure was better than the disease. But accurate knowledge developed slowly. Even in the 1890s Creighton, the author of the splendid *History of epidemics in Britain*, occasionally wrote in a vein reminiscent of Hippocrates, referring to plague, for example, as 'a typhus of the soil, or a disease made so much more malignant than typhus just because of underground fermentation of the putrescible animal matters. . .'[21]

During most of the nineteenth century improvements in health were a by-product of increases in wealth. The two went hand in hand. The age-specific death rates of the nineteenth century are amongst the most important and impressive testimonies to the economic benefits which came in the wake of the industrial revolution and which took place among the mass of the people in spite of the rapid growth of population. The long-standing connection between increasing pressure of numbers and declining real incomes per head which had marked so much of pre-industrial European history was finally broken by changes in the sources from which flowed the wealth of nations and of men. The productive powers of society could and did grow more quickly than populations so that increase of population was no longer difficult to reconcile with increasing individual prosperity. Neither fertility nor mortality was any longer density-dependent in the manner familiar to Malthus and still to be observed among wild life of all sorts.

The essentials of this story have been told so often that it is unnecessary to rehearse them here at length. The old pre-industrial economies always suffered from the fact that the production of almost all major industrial raw materials as well as food came from the land (see pages 56–9) and an increasing supply could in most cases only be obtained at the cost of declining marginal returns. Whether new and poorer land was brought into cultivation or the land already in use was cultivated more intensively this tended to hold true. This in turn depressed real incomes (and might bring in its train other troubles such as soil exhaustion and erosion).

During the industrial revolution in as much as economies continued to be based upon the raw materials produced from the soil the problem of declining marginal returns was solved in two ways. In the first place it was solved in the only way which enables the iron logic of decreasing marginal returns to be circumvented – by the flow of new inventions, technical improvements, better use of labour, better educated labour, and so on. It is difficult to give quantitative expression to this at so early a date, but it is interesting to note that a recent calculation suggests that seven-eighths of the increase in productivity per head and hence in real incomes which has taken place in the last half-century in the United States may be attributed to human ingenuity in this fashion rather than to any increase in the amount of capital employed.[22] The changes in agricultural practice already touched upon (see pages 168–9) did not simply give a single boost to agricultural productivity. On the contrary further developments in technique have set back repeatedly the point at which decreasing returns must allegedly set in. As a result each acre of land yields far more today than a century and a half ago and yet requires the labour of only a fraction of the former labour force. In round terms British farmers today supply a half of the food requirements of 55 million people, though the total number of men employed on the land is only about 800,000. In 1801 a work force more than twice as large (1·7 millions)[23] supplied the needs of population of only $10\frac{1}{2}$ millions. Comparisons of productivity over such a long period of time are seldom very satisfactory, but the obvious deduction that one man employed on the land today produces five or six times as much food as his predecessor did at the beginning of the nineteenth century is certainly an underestimate since it takes no account of the increase in the quality and quantity of food intake per head. And much the same story could, of course, be told of the agricultures of other European countries.

The settlement of new lands overseas provided a second way of escape from the problem of declining marginal returns, the extensive solution to the old dilemma. In this way also greater production could be won without causing unit costs of production to rise. Indeed each improvement in transport and each new machine devised to reduce the labour requirements of agriculture made food and other agricultural raw materials available more and more cheaply.

The changes in industry were even more spectacular than those in agriculture and tend to catch the eye more if only because they were concentrated in limited areas whose whole appearance was radically altered. In industry there were in many cases increasing marginal returns to scale because as demand grew, more efficient means of large-scale production could be adopted. With the use of water or steam power and the concentration of production in the factory rather than the home, for example, the unit cost of production of cotton goods fell considerably as the scale of production grew. Cotton piece goods became both cheaper and better in quality decade by decade in England after the first great surge of production based on new methods in the 1780s. The whole process was self-reinforcing. If real incomes grew, demand for industrial products grew. If the scale of production increased, the cost of making the article declined. This in turn would tend to raise the real value of wages and so increase demand. The old cut-off mechanism which had bedevilled periods of industrial expansion in the past, when demand lost impetus as real wages fell due to population pressure and declining marginal returns in a land-orientated economy, was now eliminated. Positive feedback had replaced negative feedback. Real incomes did not now decline when population grew (or more accurately did not come under increasing pressure as population growth gathered momentum; on the contrary the only period when the movement of real wages in England is in serious doubt lies in the *first* decades of the nineteenth century, before the industrial revolution had fully established itself). Nor did the growth of industry multiply the pressure on the land by adding an increased demand for organic industrial raw materials to the increased demand for food. Most industry was now based on minerals, and above all coal (see pages 56–9). The supply of mineral raw materials also generates certain characteristic problems but the flow of invention has so far withstood them with ease.

Fertility and the demographic transition

The effects upon mortality or the improved living standards made possible by the industrial revolution have now been described. What were their effects upon fertility?

Like so many other aspects of demographic history a satisfactory answer to this question must await much further research, but one fact of over-riding importance stands out. In time the control of conception within marriage became very widespread and fertility rates fell to levels in all probability lower than any to be found in any previous period. Any population which before the industrial revolution had displayed such low fertility rates would have disappeared quickly from the face of the earth.

In many pre-industrial populations it is reasonable to think of fertility as, in a sense, the pace-setter. Where fertility levels were very high, so also were mortality levels, and they were high because of the pressure caused by high fertility. There were levels below which mortality would not fall whatever the level of fertility, of course, set by the prevalent types of disease and by other factors, but fertility was often well above this level and tended to drag up mortality rates in sympathy because of the inability of pre-industrial economies to absorb steady population increase. After the industrial revolution, on the other hand, it might be said that mortality was the pace-setter. Production grew more quickly than population so that death rates were no longer forced to remain close to birth rates by a Malthusian ceiling. Fertility has not always fallen in step with mortality, of course, but the steady fall in mortality rates created a situation in which fertility could also fall without causing numbers to shrink. And there proved to be both personal and social pressures in the new situation created by the lower death rates which eventually led to much smaller families and the widespread practice of contraception.

Although the gross result of the industrial revolution is clear, it would be misleading to suggest that it represented a complete break with the past. There were English communities in the seventeenth century which practised family limitation (see page 124), and family limitation became widespread in France during the late eighteenth and early nineteenth centuries among populations whose lives had been very little if at all changed by the industrial revolution (for example, Crulai in Normandy; Sainghin-en-Mélantois in the Nord department; or a group of three small parishes near Auneuil in the Beauvaisis). If the right 'triggers' were present family limitation could clearly be important in a pre-industrial setting. The industrial revolution merely created conditions conducive to the adoption of family limitation upon an unprecedented scale.

Paradoxically, the immediate effect of the industrial revolution on fertility rates in the industrial areas was to push them up rather than down. But it is essential not to suppose that the short-term effects were necessarily like the long. Table 5·11, for example, shows what happened in the chief Ruhr areas in the second half of the nineteenth century. Münster provides a particularly vivid illustration of the degree of change which could occur when a new area was engulfed by a rapidly growing industrial region. Coal mining spread very rapidly in *Kreis* Recklinghausen in the south of Münster from the early 1870s. The general fertility rate rose by almost half (47 per cent) between 1860 and 1900 and even the marital fertility rate, which is not affected by changes in the sex ratios and the proportions married, rose by 15 per cent between 1870 and 1900. The other areas were already partially industrialised even by 1860. In them general fertility rose less spectacularly and marital fertility was already at a peak in 1870 – the average rate in Arnsberg, Düsseldorf and Aachen being 16 per cent above the national average at that time. The importance of the sex ratio and of religious adherence in German populations of the period,

Table 5·11 Marital and general fertility rates in Germany in the later nineteenth century [24]

Marital fertility	1860–2	1870–2	1879–81	1899–1901	1909–11
Arnsberg		352	351	346	277
Düsseldorf		363	358	325	243
Aachen		379	381	373	307
Münster		331	347	380	350
Prussia		**314**	**314**	**290**	**239**
General fertility					
Arnsberg	174	195	204	204	168
Düsseldorf	162	175	181	171	136
Aachen	147	160	166	160	137
Münster	127	137	155	187	185
Prussia	**165**	**164**	**168**	**160**	**134**

Note
Marital fertility: total legitimate children born per annum per 1,000 married women 15–44.
General fertility: total children born per annum per 1,000 women 15–44.

incidentally, is very well brought out by comparing the marital and general fertility rates in Aachen and Arnsberg. Marital fertility was consistently higher in Aachen but general fertility was very much lower, indeed below the Prussian average until the end of the century. This was partly due to religion – Catholic areas tended to marry later (Aachen was solidly Catholic, Arnsberg predominantly Protestant); and partly due to the sex ratio in the two areas – Arnsberg, a heavy industrial area, had a big surplus of men in the young adult age groups, whereas in Aachen, which had an important woollen industry affording much employment for women, the numbers were roughly equal.

Some of the complexities which make the interpretation of statistics like those in table 5·11 so difficult have already been discussed (see pages 158–61 and 164). Unusual sex ratios among young adults may raise general fertility rates substantially by encouraging early marriage for women. Marital fertility rates may be raised by the spread of different suckling habits appropriate to the new social and economic environment. High infant mortality rates may produce a spurious, if slight, positive effect on fertility; and so on. Crude birth rates demand even more cautious handling since a change in the age structure of a population can cause large but misleading rises in the crude birth rate while more discriminating measures of fertility would show no change (and the new industrial areas usually attracted a large number of young adult immigrants). Nor should the constant interplay between mortality and fertility be overlooked. If mortality rates in the fertile age-groups fall significantly, fewer marriages will be broken by death before the end of the wife's fertile period and as a result fertility will rise. Whatever the difficulties of interpretation and explanation, however, it is evident that general fertility rates rose considerably in the Ruhr in the new industrial areas, and much the same story could be told of similar areas in the Nord and Pas-de-Calais in France or of the English coalfield industrial areas.

A combination of continued high fertility rates with declining child mortality produced the Victorian family. large by legend (except of course in France) and probably larger in fact than European families for many centuries. It was not so much the completed family size in the demographic sense which grew (that is the number of live children borne by women married at a given age by the end of their child-bearing period), as what might be called the existential family, the number of children living together with their parents in a family unit. With many fewer child deaths, fewer marriages broken by the early death of a parent, and in some areas a rise in fertility as well, children grew up in larger sibling groups. It is possible that the custom of putting children out to service while still very young may have declined, and if so this would also have tended to increase the size of the existential family.

Rates of natural increase in the nineteenth century tended to be high by earlier standards, except in France (though comparison of table 5·12 with table 5·1 shows that the eighteenth century was quite 'modern' in this respect). In several countries rates of natural increase were close to one per cent per annum (a rate of growth which implies a doubling of the population in about 70 years). The rates in table 5·12 are rates of total increase and since emigration from some countries (notably Italy in the second half of the century) was heavy, they understate the rates of natural increase.

The stage was set for the steady spread of methods of limiting conception within the family. Societies as a whole were no longer threatened by a change of this sort because of the fall in mortality which continued steadily. Individuals might often benefit from it since it enabled them to enjoy a higher effective standard of living than would otherwise have been possible, and to ensure that the upbringing of the early children in the family was not threatened by the arrival in the world of too large a number of younger brothers and sisters.

The restriction of fertility which took place was in an important sense a return to an earlier pattern. Before the industrial revolution in most periods of history the size of any one generation was not much different from that of its predecessor or successor, and roughly the same number of children survived to marriageable age

Table 5·12 Population growth in nineteenth-century Europe [25]

	Population size (millions)			Percentage growth rates per annum	
	1800	1850	1900	1800–50	1850–1900
Russia	40	57	100	0·71	1·14
Germany	23	35	56	0·84	0·95
Italy	18	25	33	0·66	0·53
France	28	36	41	0·47	0·25
Great Britain	11	21	37	1·30	1·14

in each generation. Since a few people in each generation do not marry this implies that just over two children per family in the siblings' generation reached adult years. To achieve this, of course, might mean giving birth to twice as many children because of the high level of mortality early in life. The spread of family limitation since the later nineteenth century has gradually restored this position (though at different times in the last forty years in many western countries the pendulum has swung a little to one side or the other of simple replacement of one generation by the next). Viewed in this way it was the intervening period of rapid growth in the eighteenth and nineteenth centuries when each new generation was considerably larger than its predecessor on reaching adult years that was unusual.

The onset of family limitation had certain common features in most European countries. In general it was evident first and went furthest among the rich, the well-educated, the upper class. There was for many years after contraception was first widely practised a strong inverse correlation between income and family size. As the decades passed those lower down the social pyramid began to

Table 5·13 The fall in family size in Great Britain by socio-economic groups[26]

	Professional	Employers	Own account	Salaried Employees	Non-manual wage earners
1890–9	2·80	3·28	3·70	3·04	3·53
1900–9	2·33	2·64	2·96	2·37	2·89
1915	2·02	2·07	2·13	1·88	2·20
1925	1·69	1·71	1·82	1·48	1·77
All groups = 100					
1890–9	65	76	85	70	81
1900–9	66	75	84	67	82
1915	77	79	82	72	84
1925	75	76	81	66	79

Note Live births to all completed marriages in which the wife was under 45 at marriage. The dates refer to the years in which the marriages were contracted.

follow the lead of the upper echelons but the relative differences in family size remained strongly marked for a long time. Table 5·13 shows the changes which occurred in Great Britain. Sizes fell very substantially in all groups but the relative differences were very stable. The only groups to alter much in this respect were the two which in the earliest period were the furthest apart. The family size of labourers fell less rapidly than that of other groups so that their index number rose from 118 to 136. The 1925 cohort produced families more than twice as large as those of the salaried employees. The professional group, on the other hand, moved nearer to the average. Here too family size fell less rapidly than in other groups.

The 1961 census produced clear evidence that the fertility differentials between the chief socio-economic groups in England and Wales have narrowed considerably in recent years. They also suggest that the smallest families may now increasingly be found in the middle income range with larger families among the better off as well as among the poorer classes. Marriages which have been

	Manual wage earners	Farmers and farm managers	Agri-cultural workers	Labour-ers	All groups
1890–9	4·85	4·30	4·71	5·11	4·34
1900–9	3·96	3·50	3·88	4·45	3·53
1915	2·91	2·69	2·74	3·54	2·61
1925	2·48	2·22	2·62	3·05	2·24
All groups = 100					
1890–9	112	99	109	118	100
1900–9	112	99	110	126	100
1915	111	103	105	136	100
1925	111	99	117	136	100

in existence for as long as 25 years very seldom produce further children. Therefore, the figures in columns **C** and **D** of table 5·14 are for completed families. In every case the more recent families started in the early 1930s are smaller than the older families. The families in column **B** are not in all cases complete since some were only ten years old. It is therefore particularly interesting to note that in several cases families in this column were already larger on average than the completed families of column **C**. The ratios in column **E** show that the groups which previously had the largest families – manual workers and agricultural workers – had relatively the smallest families, while family sizes were rising in professional, managerial and some clerical groups. Fertility differentials had shrunk considerably. The ratio of the largest to the smallest family size in column **D** is as 177:100. In column **B** it is only as 137:100. In both cases the highest figure is found in the unskilled manual group, but the lowest figure in column **B** is the junior non-manual group, a group very differently placed both socially and economically from the group which is smallest in column **D**, professional employees. It is interesting to note, incidentally, that the column **B** figure for the self-employed professional group is substantially larger not only than that in column **C** but also than that in column **D**. One would probably have to go back to a marriage cohort formed in the nineteenth century to find a family size for this group as large after 10–14 years of marriage as that found in 1961.

France stands apart from other European countries in nineteenth-century demographic history. Her population grew much less than other countries because family limitation was widespread in rural communities in many parts of France from very early in the century. Peasant families were often very modest in size. The fall in fertility took place at the same time as the fall in mortality, and not after an interval of half a century as in other countries. The adoption of family limitation in France was often accompanied by a very interesting change in marriage patterns. Once fertility in marriage could be controlled couples married earlier and those areas in which marital fertility fell earliest and most were also those in which the proportions of men and women who were married in the young age-groups rose first and furthest. Marital fertility in Aisne in 1860–2, for example, was 165 per 1,000. In Finisterre it was 309 (87 per cent higher). But the numbers of women ever married per 1,000 total population in 1861 in the age-groups 20–4, 25–9, and 30–4 in Aisne were 506, 787 and 875 respectively, whereas in Finisterre they were only 269, 516 and 726. As a result general fertility rates were much less far apart than marital fertility rates; in Aisne 114 per 1,000, in Finisterre 142 (25 per cent higher).[27] It was as if being relieved of the burden of unrestrained fertility allowed populations to give rein much earlier to the 'passion between the sexes'. The mechanism of social adjustment here is a fascinating field for further study.

When family size began to be deliberately limited in western Europe in the nineteenth century, the result was achieved largely by 'pre-industrial' methods, by *coitus interruptus* and by the procuring of abortions, both means which had been available to

Table 5·14 Family sizes in England and Wales by socio-economic groups and duration of marriage in 1961[28]

Length of marriage (years)	A 5	B 10–14	C 25–9	D 40–44	E Ratio of B to C
Employers and managers — large establishments	1·27	1·81	1·68	1·86	108
Employers and managers — small establishments	1·34	1·78	1·77	1·94	101
Professional — self-employed	1·66	2·17	1·86	1·98	117
Professional — employees	1·39	1·86	1·68	1·75	111
Intermediate non-manual	1·25	1·76	1·66	1·94	106
Junior non-manual	1·20	1·68	1·68	2·14	100
Personal service workers	1·37	1·90	1·97	2·29	96
Foremen and supervisors — manual	1·27	1·90	1·95	2·42	97
Skilled manual	1·39	2·00	2·12	2·55	94
Semi-skilled manual	1·49	2·02	2·19	2·78	92
Unskilled manual	1·71	2·30	2·46	3·10	93
Own account (non-prof.)	1·45	1·88	1·79	2·20	105
Farmer — employers and managers	1·62	2·22	2·27	2·56	98
Farmer — own account	1·48	1·99	1·97	2·59	101
Agricultural workers	1·54	2·10	2·38	3·02	88
All groups	**1·40**	**1·94**	**2·01**	**2·47**	**97**

Note Live births to women married once only at an age less than 45 and enumerated with their husbands.

societies for centuries previously. The use of rubber sheaths and caps and spermicidal chemicals, which might be called 'post-industrial' methods of family limitation, played a comparatively minor role until well into the twentieth century. Lewis-Faning found evidence that in England only 16 per cent of those women living in the late 1940s whose marriage had been contracted before 1910, and who had practised birth control, had used appliance methods. The percentage rose slowly. For those married 1920–4 the figure was 31 per cent, rising to 57 per cent for those married 1940–7.[29] The alternative method principally used was *coitus interruptus*. In the main, therefore, the tremendous growth in the use of contraception to limit family size from the late nineteenth century onwards was due to the much wider employment of means long known to European societies rather than to the opportunities afforded to them by the development of new techniques. The changes in marital fertility would have followed much the same path in all probability even if no new techniques of control had been invented.

The motives which caused individual couples to begin to limit their families are still far from clear. In the past explanations have usually been sought in the sphere of the economic self-interest either of the individual or the family. Le Play, for example, believed that the great fall in fertility among the French peasantry occurred because under the provisions of the *Code civil* the small proprietor was virtually obliged to divide his estate among his offspring equally. He supposed peasants to dislike the subdivision of their holdings sufficiently strongly to try to keep their families small.[30] Or again, it has been argued that when the English middle classes began to practise contraception in the 1870s this was because they were under severe economic pressure.[31] Consumption habits had been acquired during the long period of preceding prosperity which could be maintained only with great difficulty, but which could be abandoned only at the cost of an intolerable loss of face socially. Caught thus in a scissors between increasingly expensive consumption habits and stagnant or falling incomes they could alleviate matters in many cases by reducing expenditure on children.

More generally the argument is put in the form that populations which were in general both wealthier and better educated were much more keenly alive to the penalties which had to be paid by each family for increasing its size. The industrial revolution not only put more money into most men's pockets but created in them the expectation of a secular rise in living standards and therefore a secular improvement in the range and quality of consumer goods which most families could afford. This ensured both a clearer appreciation of the advantages of small families and a more flexible social milieu in which family limitation methods could spread. The argument has some similarity to de Tocqueville's classic analysis of revolutionary outbreaks. Only those who are somewhat better off than their fathers and in whom the expectation of further improvement has been awakened are likely to revolt if living conditions suddenly worsen since only they have a clear appreciation of the delights of further progress. Similarly only those who have known rising real incomes and have enjoyed the benefits which they bring are sufficiently alive to the advantages which accompany a reduction in family size to act positively to restrict the number of their children (and it is noteworthy that family size began to fall in most countries in the 1870s and 1880s, a generation after average real incomes had started to move decisively upwards – in many countries this began about 1850). This may help also to explain why the worst off do least and do it last.

Alternatively, it might be said that the situation which previously obtained on the scale of the society as a whole was transferred to that of the family. In pre-industrial times increasing population tended to mean declining real incomes per head. After the industrial revolution this was no longer the case on the scale of the whole society because the increase in production more than kept pace with the increase in population. But within any individual family matters were much as they had previously been for the society as a whole. The family's cash income was not increased by the arrival of a new child, but each new mouth to feed and body to clothe meant a reduction of expenditure in other directions. Accordingly, whereas before the industrial revolution many societies appear to have developed sanctions which tended to restrict fertility, for example against early marriage, after the industrial revolution social sanctions gradually disappeared but family sanctions grew.

In general form these arguments are difficult to resist. They must have much truth in them. In more particular settings there are often difficulties. Events seldom fall out as neatly as models of social and individual action suggest. And even when events do fit the suggested patterns quite well there is frequently some difficulty in understanding just what the trigger mechanism was which started up a new pattern of behaviour. For example, the argument from the *Code civil* through economic self-interest and a sense of the importance of an undivided holding to family limitation among the French peasantry does only rather rough justice to the facts, since family limitation was already beginning to appear in some districts before the *Code* was promulgated. Some French areas, and notably Brittany, though the population contained many peasants, did not show large falls in marital fertility until several generations later, Moreover, there were other countries with similar codes in which fertility fell only much later in the nineteenth century. Belgium is a particularly interesting instance of this for there the Walloon and Flemish areas behaved quite differently.

The British middle classes in the 1870s were not experiencing the problem of 'keeping up with the Joneses' for the first time, nor is there much reason to suppose that their difficulties then were more acute than in some previous periods of strain. The Genevan bourgeoisie had restricted their families drastically and effectively as much as two hundred years before. Why then should the 1870s have proved capable of triggering off changes when earlier crises had not? The full answer to this question must inevitably be complex and is unlikely to be solely a matter of economic pressure.

Overhanging all the special problems of family limitation in particular settings, there is the general conundrum why family limitation should have begun to be practised on a scale large enough to affect national or regional fertility rates almost simultaneously across much of Europe in spite of the very different levels of economic advance and the variegated social circumstances prevailing. The variations of a decade or two in the timing of the onset of the decline in marital fertility rates which occur are surprisingly slight in view of the considerable regional differences in the rate of social and economic change generally. The English case appears to have been typical of most other European countries, and therefore what happened in England may serve as an example of the timing and extent of the revolution which took place (always excepting France).

Figure 5·4 and table 5·15 show the fluctuations in the crude birth rate and in general and marital fertility which have taken place since 1851. The highest point in all three occurred in the decade 1871–80. The lowest point in the first two series was reached in 1936–40. The lowest point in marital fertility, on the other hand, occurred in 1951–5 when the rate was slightly lower than in either 1941–5 or 1936–40, the two next lowest periods. The crude birth rate fell 58 per cent, general fertility 60 per cent and marital fertility 64 per cent between the highest and lowest points in their respective series. The fact that general fertility fell less far than marital fertility reflects the growing percentage of married women in the fertile age-groups (this trend has been heavily underlined in recent years: between 1936–40 and 1962 general fertility rose 49 per cent whereas marital fertility rose only 16 per cent, the difference being due to the great fall in the proportion of unmarried women of child-bearing age). Marital fertility is the measure amongst these three which most directly reflects the extent of the practice of contraception and the immensity of the change involved is well brought out by the fact that the marital fertility rate fell by almost two-thirds in three-quarters of a century.

The gross reproduction rates shown in table 5·16 (for definition see pages 20–1) restate the same changes in fertility in a different way. They show how many daughters on an average would be born to each woman given the fertility rates prevailing at the date in question. Naturally the timing and the amount of the fall is very

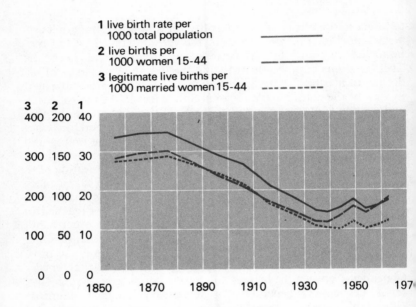

1 live birth rate per
  1000 total population

2 live births per
  1000 women 15-44

3 legitimate live births per
  1000 married women 15-44

similar to that of the general fertility rate. The gross reproduction rate fell below unity in the 1930s and had fertility continued at that level the population must have fallen even if there had been no wastage of life between birth and maturity. The net reproduction rate fell much less than the gross, of course, (by only 50 per cent compared with 63 per cent 1871–1933) because of the steady improvement in child mortality and later in infant mortality. The gross and net rates moved steadily closer together as the years passed and the waste of young life dwindled. By 1963 the net reproduction rate was only three per cent lower than the gross whereas in 1841 it was a full 40 per cent lower. Indeed by 1963 the net rate was almost as high as it had been in 1841 whereas the gross rate was only about three-fifths as high.

All the fertility measures used so far are measures of current

Table 5·15 The fall in fertility in England and Wales in the last century[32]

	Live birth rate per 1,000 total population	Live births per 1,000 women 15–44	Legitimate live births per 1,000 married women 15–44
1851–60	34·1	144·9	281·0
1861–70	35·2	151·0	287·3
1871–80	35·4	153·6	295·5
1881–90	32·4	138·7	274·6
1891–1900	29·9	122·7	250·3
1901–10	27·2	109·0	221·6
1911–20	21·8	87·7	173·5
1921–30	18·3	73·9	143·6
1931–5	15·0	61·7	115·2
1936–40	14·7	60·9	107·3
1941–5	15·9	69·3	105·4
1946–50	18·0	80·9	122·5
1951–5	15·2	72·5	105·0
1956–60	16·3	81·8	113·4
1961–3	17·8	90·5	123·7

Table 5·16 Gross and net reproduction rates in England and Wales since 1841[33]

	GRR	NRR			GRR	NRR
1841	2·237	1·349		1923	1·153	0·966
1851	2·264	1·381		1933	0·862	0·756
1861	2·277	1·427		1938	0·897	0·805
1871	2·356	1·511		1939–49	1·031	0·945
1881	2·252	1·511		1950–4	1·061	1·015
1891	1·973	1·369		1960	1·291	1·252
1901	1·702	1·238		1963	1·389	1·347
1911	1·428	1·121				

Note The figures down to 1933 are three-year averages. Thereafter they are for individual years or are annual averages.

performance and may fluctuate quite sharply in response to special circumstances which last only a short time. For example, current rates may fall sharply during a period of depression and unemployment because couples postpone having further children until economic conditions improve, and yet the final size of their families may remain unaffected. Similarly there is often a bunching of births in the year or two immediately after a war when the soldiers return home. And even if there are no perturbations of this sort in current rates, they are still apt to be misleading. When, for example, there is a female gross reproduction rate of 2·00 this means that the average woman would bear two female children, *assuming the current age-specific rates to continue throughout her fertile life*. But a woman may bear children over a period of more than 20 years, and age-specific rates will change greatly over two decades when contraception is becoming more and more widely practised. A young woman of 20 belonging to a generation (in demographic jargon a cohort) which has begun to limit its families will not when she reaches the age of 35 be as likely to have a child as an older sister in a different cohort with different habits who is already 35, but a gross reproduction rate calculated from current age-specific rates cannot tell us this. What can, and what is therefore a valuable further perspective on the revolutionary change in patterns of family formation is a cohort measure such as that in table 5.17. In this table the decline in family size of women married at or between certain dates is given. For example, women married 1861–9 had an average of 6·16 children during their fertile lives – the last of these being born, of course, in the late 1880s or early 1890s.

Table 5·17 and figure 5·5 show that family size was falling from the 1860s onwards and that it fell rapidly from the cohort of 1871 until the cohort of 1925–9. Thereafter the decline bottomed out and indeed with the crop of marriages immediately after the Second World War the trend was reversed. The total fall in family size between the cohort of 1861–9 and the cohort of 1935–9 was almost exactly two-thirds (67 per cent). The decline was notably regular (and remains so even if cohorts of single years are used)

Figure 5·5 The decline in family size in England and Wales from 1861 (for further details see note to table 5·17).

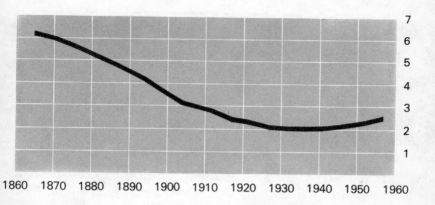

Table 5·17 The decline in family size by marriage cohorts in England and Wales from 1861[34]

	Family size		Family size		Family size
1861–9	6·16	1900–9	3·30	1935–9	2·04
1871	5·94	1910–14	2·82	1940–4	2·08
1876	5·62	1915–19	2·46	1945–9	2·20
1881	5·27	1920–4	2·31	1950–4	2·31
1886	4·81	1925–9	2·11	1955–9	2·55
1890–9	4·13	1930–4	2·07		

Note Mean ultimate family size of marriages contracted when woman under 45. Down to the 1925–9 cohort all family formation has been completed and the figures are therefore reliable. For the cohorts 1930–44 formation is virtually complete and the figures are therefore reliable. Thereafter an increasingly large proportion of total family formation has not been completed. The later fertility of these cohorts has been estimated using the 1962–3 current fertility rates. All the quinquennial figures from 1910 onwards are averages of annual figures.

Table 5.18 The relative frequency of families of different sizes in Great Britain, 1870–1925[35]

Number of births	Marriage cohorts 1870–9	1890–9	1900–9	1915	1925
0	83	99	113	150	161
1	53	95	148	212	252
2	72	136	187	235	254
3	86	136	157	159	144
4	95	122	120	95	77
5	95	100	84	59	45
6	94	83	63	35	27
7	89	65	45	21	18
8	83	52	32	15	10
9	73	40	22	9	6
10	62	30	15	6	4
11 plus	115	42	14	4	2
	1,000	1,000	1,000	1,000	1,000

Note: Live birth to completed marriages contracted when woman was under 45.

and so was the later rise. The 'baby booms' after the two great wars which boosted measures very markedly for a year or two clearly did not affect the underlying trend of family formation, only the timing of individual births. It is also noteworthy that the marriages begun in the late 1860s and early 1870s must already have included couples who limited the size of their families, though the current fertility measures were all rising to a peak at that time. If we wish to identify the first marriage cohorts to use birth control to an appreciable extent, we must look back to a date before the current rates were at their highest.

Perhaps the most revealing of all the ways of breaking down the statistics of the spread of birth control through the population is shown in table 5·18. This makes clear how the strategy of family formation changed during the period when fertility fell so drastically. In the 1870–9 cohort of marriages a one-child family was less likely to occur than a ten-child family and one family in nine had 11 or more children. In the 1925 cohort a family of one was 60 times more likely to occur than a family of ten and hardly any marriages produced 11 or more children. Indeed in this cohort only one family in nine produced five or more children and just over half of all families were of one or two children. The outstanding features of the table are the remarkable bunching of families of these two sizes and the virtual disappearance of the large family of five or more children. Well might a woman in the 1930s feel herself an object of remark and sometimes even of scorn, if she were known to have even, say, four children. A statistical rarity is often a social outcast. And table 5·18 refers, of course, to all classes in the country. Since average family size differed by a factor of two between labourers (3·05) and salaried employees (1·48) in the 1925 cohort there were groups within the community in which families even of three children were uncommon, and in which a family of five was almost unknown (see table 5·13).

The history of the revolutionary change in family size brought about by couples using *coitus interruptus* and other contraceptive techniques as a normal adjunct of intercourse within marriage is in outline a comparatively straightforward affair. In the space of two generations or a little more, average family size fell by roughly two-thirds, the new pattern of behaviour being adopted first by middle and upper middle class groups within the general population – lawyers, doctors or businessmen – and percolating down through the social pyramid to affect the habits of coalminers and agricultural labourers somewhat later. Only in the last generation have family size differentials between the different classes begun to lessen with some middle and upper middle class groups producing larger families while those least well off probably continuing the trend towards fewer children, and the smallest families of all being found where the father holds one of the less well paid clerical jobs.

Once more, however, some caution in interpreting the evidence is required. The history of family limitation in France and indeed at an earlier period in England suggests that perhaps all populations and groups within populations carry in reserve, as it were, the ability to restrict fertility within marriage whenever conditions are such as to call this into play. It is too soon to assert dogmatically that family limitation is always found earlier among the upper than the lower ranks of society. Again, the pressures within the family *milieu* which encourage family limitation are not well understood. It is to be remembered that as long as *coitus interruptus* was the main technique employed, the decision to employ contraception and limit family size was a male prerogative. The incentive to do this may have been weak in a coal mining community in which, say, the life of the married men was little affected by the size of their families because they spent the working day away from the home, the evenings in the pub, and only handed over to their wives a sum of money for housekeeping after keeping back money for their own pleasures and amusements. Where the home was also the centre of the economic activity of the family and the father spent many more of his waking hours with his family (say as a cobbler or small shopkeeper), his attitude to family limitation may have been quite different.

There may also have been important differences in the speed of adoption of family limitation between 'pure' and 'mixed' communities. Where the great bulk of the heads of households made their living from coal mining, they had little opportunity to see the changes taking place in communities in which many different social and occupational groups lived in close proximity to each other. How did the occasional service and tertiary industry households living in otherwise 'pure' communities behave? Were the families of local butchers, postmen and publicans in these areas large like those of their neighbours, or smaller like their occupational groups in the country as a whole? How closely were full literacy and length of education correlated with the early spread of family limitation? The questions of interest are numerous. The answers which can be given with confidence are remarkably few. Much information lies awaiting analysis in the census enumerators' books but unhappily in England these are not normally available to scholars until a full century has elapsed because of the so-called hundred year rule, under which census information only ceases to be confidential after one hundred years have elapsed. The practice in other countries, incidentally, varies considerably. For example, in Holland all the original census schedules are destroyed once the information on them has been abstracted for the census tabulations. In France, the original census schedules remain confidential for 50 years, though access to more recent census materials may be obtained for research purposes (on the other hand civil registration documents remain confidential for a full hundred years).

One final general characteristic of all populations which have lived through the industrial revolution may be remarked. Although the immediate upheaval of society and disruption of old communities often produced striking and at times shocking variations in mortality, and although the spread of family limitation through post-industrial societies produced for a time big differences within the community in fertility and family size, it seems safe to advance it as a general rule that these differences within society grow less and less.

This is notably true of mortality. The large differences in age-specific mortality by social class have shrunk steadily since the middle of the nineteenth century. The enormous differences between Liverpool and Surrey which so roused Farr in his day are now much slighter. Lancashire is still a somewhat less healthy county than Surrey but the differences are no longer so large that expectation of life in the one is twice that in the other. Some large differences remain in certain mortality rates, both between different classes and different parts of the country. For example, the perinatal mortality rate (deaths in the first week of life plus stillbirths per 1,000 live and stillbirths) in Burnley in Lancashire in 1962 was twice the level in Cambridgeshire (43 and 22 per 1,000).[36] But these continuing contrasts no longer seriously affect expectation of life at birth. In western countries today mortality is everywhere tending towards what has sometimes been called the biological minimum, that is to say a position in which age-specific death rates only reflect deaths due to the degeneration of some bodily function or the working out of a genetic defect. Deaths from diseases which invade the body from without have been well nigh eliminated. Only an advance in medical science which inhibited the operation of the ageing process or provided a successful counter to diseases like those of the circulatory system could reduce mortality further to any significant degree. Expectation of life may rise to about 77 years but can hardly go higher in these circumstances.[37] It is already 73 in Norway (1951–5); 71 in New Zealand (1955–7); 73 in Holland (1956–60); and only slightly lower in larger countries. In Russia it is 70 (1960–1); in the United Kingdom 71 (1960–2); in the United States 70 (1962).[38]

Differences in fertility in different social groups are much greater relatively than those in mortality. Occasionally groups like the Hutterites in the United States may continue to maintain fertility rates at 'pre-industrial' levels, but in general the large fertility differences between the two extremes of the social scale which obtained for much of the last century have narrowed considerably in recent years, relatively as well as absolutely.

These changes have been the fruits of the industrial revolution. As a result men can now control both birth and death in a fashion which would have appeared beyond attainment for all times to men of Malthus' generation and persuasion.

6 For richer, for poorer

6 For richer, for poorer

It is often said, and with good reason, that a knowledge of the past is important to the understanding of the present. The reverse of this is also true – that it is an advantage in studying the past to have some knowledge of the present. In both cases a fuller perspective is gained. In particular, acquaintance with the demography of the world today both in the rich countries and the poor brings home the immensity of the changes set in train by the industrial revolution.

The most striking gross fact about population history in recent years is the enormous growth in numbers which has occurred. Table 6·1 and figure 6·1 show how great the growth has been, and how much it has accelerated. Populations are growing in all parts of the world at rates which were rare or unparalleled in pre-industrial times, but rates of growth are much higher in the developing countries than in western Europe and North America and are still accelerating in the former though not in the latter. In the industrialised countries fertility has fallen greatly but elsewhere it is still very high. There are comparatively few countries in an intermediate position. Population characteristics and problems, therefore, differ notably between the two major types of economy and society, and require separate consideration.

The developing countries

The most striking feature common to these countries is the tremendous fall in mortality which has taken place since the end of the Second World War. Crude death rates in the developing countries are now frequently lower than in European countries because a higher proportion of their populations is young, in age-groups where the risk of death is slight (see figure 6·2). In a number of countries expectation of life has been rising by one year or more per annum for a decade or more. In some it now approaches the level reached in industrialised countries. In Taiwan, for example, in 1959–60 it was 61 years for men and 66 for women: in Puerto

Table 6·1 The growth of population in major areas 1750–1950[2] with projections for 2000 (populations in millions)

	1750	1800	1850	1900	1950	2000
Asia	498	630	801	925	1,381	3,458
China	200	323	430	436	560	1,034
India and Pakistan	190	195	233	285	434	1,269
Africa	106	107	111	133	222	768
Europe (excluding Russia)	125	152	208	296	392	527
North America	2	7	26	82	166	354
South and Central America	16	24	38	74	162	638
Russia	42	56	76	134	180	353
Australasia and Pacific Islands	2	2	2	6	13	32
World	**791**	**978**	**1,262**	**1,650**	**2,515**	**6,130**

Rico the comparable figures in 1960 were 67 and 72 (in Great Britain in 1960–2, 68 and 74).[1]

With falling death rates and continued high fertility population growth rates have shot up. Whereas before the Second World War an annual growth rate of one per cent might have been counted high, growth rates of two or three per cent are now widespread, and

Figure 6·1 The growth of
world population 1750–1950 with
projections to 2000 (see table 6·1).
The vertical scale is logarithmic.
(population in millions).

still higher rates are sometimes found. Table 6·2 shows what such growth rates imply if continued over long periods.

Countries with high fertility and low mortality rates cannot halt their population growth overnight even if they succeed in reducing their reproduction rates abruptly. The age structure of these populations with its very high proportion of young people will entail a considerable further growth in absolute numbers even if fertility falls to the point where each generation is producing only enough children to replace itself. Ultimately the population will cease to grow but not until several further decades have elapsed.

This means, of course, that while only a fall in fertility rates in the developing countries can finally resolve the tension between numbers on the one hand and food supply or general economic development on the other, no fall in these rates, however steep, can solve the problems of the next two decades. For example, two population projections were made for India some years ago. In both mortality was assumed to fall by the same margin so that expectation of life rose from 38 years in 1956 to 52 years in 1986

Table 6·2 Sizes attained by a base population of 100 after 25, 50 and 100 years at various rates of annual increase

Rates of increase per cent per annum	After 25 years	After 50 years	After 100 years
1	128	164	270
2	164	269	724
3	209	439	1,923
4	267	710	5,047

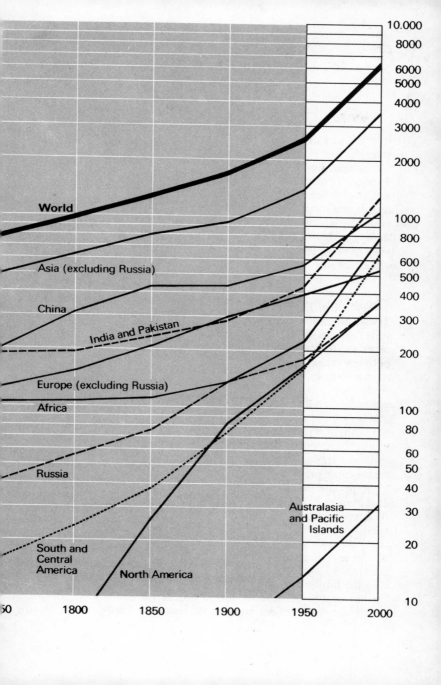

(already it seems likely that expectation of life will be much higher than 52 in 1986). In alternative **A** fertility was assumed to remain unchanged; in **B** to fall by a half evenly between the two dates. Table 6·3 shows the results.[3] Although the totals are substantially different after 30 years, they show very little difference after 10, and only a moderate difference after 20. The problems of developing countries must therefore be discussed in the knowledge that no demographic changes are likely to affect the short term situation very greatly (other than by an upward surge of mortality which would be the sign of utter failure).

The general economic problem

The rapid growth of population in the countries of Asia and Africa today poses a serious threat to economic advance because it increases the difficulty of raising real income per head. This is perhaps most simply appreciated by considering the problem of capital supply. Capital is badly needed by all developing countries to develop educational and medical services; to improve communication systems; to equip agriculture; to establish industrial plant; and so on. The list of projects in urgent need of capital is almost unending. Capital is very difficult to obtain from abroad for some of these purposes, and may prove awkward to service if export earnings are low. To raise capital at home, however, is also difficult because the great bulk of the population is very poor (see table 6·4). Poor people must spend most of their income on basic necessities and above all on food (in low income countries up to three-quarters of a typical family budget may consist of food). If a trend of rising real incomes can be established it may be confirmed into a beneficent spiral of growth if a suitable method of drawing off the bulk of the increased income into capital projects can be devised (for example by a tax system which brings a steadily rising flow of funds into the hands of the government). Then real incomes can rise still further and a positive feedback process is established. Both consumption expenditures and capital spending may now rise steadily.

Table 6·3 Two projections of India's population
(populations in millions)

	A	B
1956	384	384
1966	473	458
1976	601	531
1986	775	589

Note The population of India in 1966 was approximately 495 millions.

Table 6·4 Estimated consumption per head in 1960 in various
countries (United Kingdom = 100) [4]

United States	140	Mexico	22	Ghana	8
Sweden	125	Mauritius	16	Korean Republic	6
United Kingdom	100	Taiwan	12	India	5
West Germany	86	Ceylon	9	Pakistan	4
Algeria	22				

If, on the other hand, real incomes fail to rise or actually fall this will gravely prejudice any chance of general economic growth. Food requirements are relatively inflexible. If a man's income is low already and he spends three-quarters of it on food, and if his circumstances change for the worse, and his income falls by, say, a tenth, then the proportion of his income which he spends on food

Figure 6·2 The fall in crude death rates in developing countries (per 1000 total population). Birth rates are also shown (quinquennial until 1960).[5] Note the widening gap between birth and death rates, though birth rates have shown some tendency to fall recently in Mauritius and Barbados.

must rise, and the amount left over for any other purposes must fall sharply. Indeed, to take the limiting case, if his demand for food were incapable of any reduction and he continued to spend 75 units of income on food out of a total income which had fallen from 100 to 90 units, then the amount left over to meet all other needs would fall from 25 to 15 units, a drop of 40 per cent.

The rate of population growth materially affects a country's chances of stepping on to the beneficent spiral. Assume, for example, that the marginal capital-output ratio is about 3:1, and that therefore an annual net investment of about 10 per cent will increase national income by some 3 per cent per annum. If population is stationary or growing slowly, each year will see a gain in real income per head and cumulatively over a generation real incomes will roughly double. But if population also is growing at 3 per cent per annum there will be no improvement in living standards, and if population growth exceeds this rate living standards will fall. Since in most developing countries rates of population growth have risen sharply in the last two decades and net investment rates can be raised only with great difficulty, it is no wonder that the Red Queen's words spring to mind: 'Now, *here*, you see, it takes all *you* can do, to keep in the same place. If you want to get somewhere else, you must run at least twice as fast as that!'.

It is very doubtful whether either the particular dread of mass starvation or the general fear that population growth will inhibit economic development are properly conceived if stated as baldly as in the last few paragraphs. Political, psychological, sociological and physiological changes have taken place or are in train in the developing countries which make it unwise to rest any analysis upon abstract economic categories.

Attitudes to the gaining of a livelihood may alter as the pressures brought about by these changes rise. The threat of starvation and declining living standards may bring with it a willingness to experiment with new techniques. For this reason Boserup goes so far as to claim that '. . . primitive communities with sustained population growth have a better chance to get into a process of genuine

birth rate   death rate

Mexico

Mauritius

Barbados

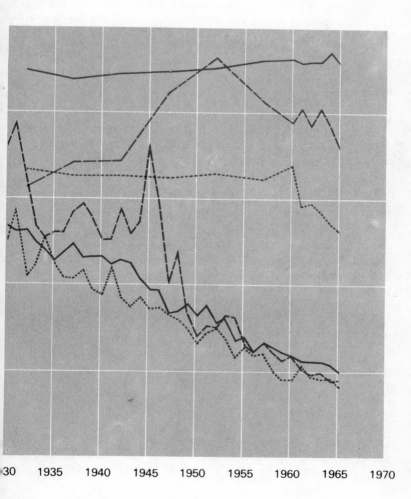

30   1935   1940   1945   1950   1955   1960   1965   1970

economic development than primitive communities with stagnant or declining populations, provided of course, that the necessary agricultural investments are undertaken'.[6] The backwardness of agriculture may even be a blessing in disguise. Quite small capital investments can produce startling increases in productivity if individual peasants can be convinced of the need for rapid and radical change. Now that mortality is low and population increase fast, not all men can hope simply to succeed in due course to the niches vacated for them by deaths in the older generation. Reactions in these circumstances may vary but it is conceivable that the challenge of population growth may act as a catalyst of change and development, though it is also possible that increased misery may induce apathy.

Again, in the particular question of food supply, it is important that in some major food producing countries the task of the agricultural ministry is more often to prevent over-production of food than to ensure that enough is grown. Millions of tons of grain are normally held in store in the United States, Canada and Australia and this provides a buffer against starvation for countries suffering from inadequate harvests. If reserves of foreign exchange are too low to make ordinary commercial arrangements practicable, political considerations will often ensure that deficiencies stop some way short of sheer starvation. The receiving countries pay a price but it is political rather than financial.

Further, the conquest of disease which brings with it problems of rapid population growth also produces countervailing advantages. A healthy man is an alert man. He is both better able to work hard and more likely to appreciate the potential benefits of change. Lives saved by the control of malaria or sleeping sickness are different in quality as well as in quantity from lives when these diseases and others like them were rife.

Even in purely economic terms the effects of rapid population increase may be favourable as long as the total volume of demand for goods rises (this it may well do even though it rises less fast than population). If the total volume of demand is rising there may be opportunities for entrepreneurs attracted by the expanding market with its promise of economies to scale. This argument, however, must be employed with great discretion. It is significant that Coale and Hoover in their study of Indian prospects concluded that with a lower rate of population growth not only would income per head grow much more quickly but that total production would also rise faster.[7] And Leibenstein places a much greater emphasis on the stimulus afforded by growing income per head than on increasing aggregate demand, especially in encouraging entrepreneurship.[8] In the main it is fair to assume that if population growth is to be beneficial it should also be moderate in pace. In most developing countries the halving of population growth rates would be an immense boon in the fight to raise living standards.

Favourable and unfavourable factors

The general situation in a developing country which is experiencing rapid population growth is sure to be, for a time at least, a complex balance of difficulties and opportunities. On the debit side of the balance there are the problems immediately highlighted by orthodox economic analysis, especially the awkward implications of any sustained period of declining real incomes per head. To this must be added the random, but formidable dangers of harvest failure, and the problems springing from the attitudes of the ruling *élites*, who may be opposed to rapid change (consciously or not), or who, though convinced of the need for change, are incompetent to push it through. On the credit side of the ledger may be set the immensely rich storehouse of technology which the advances achieved elsewhere have put at the disposal of the developing countries. The very population increases which create so many problems are the result of importing medical and public health methods from overseas. In many other fields of endeavour from education to the working of the land (and including the control of fertility) there are effective techniques available to those who hope to transform these countries, not all of them prohibitively expensive.

Better education is perhaps the surest if not the swiftest way to solve development problems. Fortunately, educational advance, though sometimes slow, is almost everywhere regarded as good so that its further progress seems assured. In many countries, it is true, a high proportion of children still go without primary education, and only a small fraction of the population of school age reaches the secondary level (for example, in India in 1955–6 only half the children aged 6–10 were enrolled at school and a fifth of those 11–13).[9] University education is attained only by a tiny handful, many of whom emigrate to industrialised countries which reward their special skills more highly. It is also true that although university educated men and women in all countries appear to adopt the 'western' small family pattern, a primary or even a secondary education does not necessarily lead to much change in this respect.[10] Education helps, however, to change other demographic characteristics. The well educated appreciate the importance of good hygiene and a balanced diet, for example, which have a great importance for health. And education helps to undermine the habit of marrying off girls at or close to puberty – the fuller the education, the later the marriage. But the effect of education upon the demography of a community is only a small part of its significance for developing countries because educated men and women are quicker to accept new methods and to use them effectively. They tend also to become more mobile both socially and geographically. These are all characteristics which in turn are intimately bound up with the engendering of economic growth.

The rapid growth of cities is another change which tends to modify traditional demographic and general social habits. Urban populations in developing countries do not always or immediately adopt the small family habits of urban populations in industrialised countries. In Puerto Rico, for example, in the early 1950s low fertility was much more clearly correlated with educational attainment than city life.[11] In India, too, there is good reason to doubt whether urban fertility is any lower than rural.[12] Nevertheless when falls in fertility occur they usually appear first and go furthest in cities (see Hong Kong and Singapore in table 6·5 below). Attitudes giving rise to high fertility are more likely to weaken in the city than in the countryside. The difficulty of educating all the children in a large family is one common pressure to which city dwellers tend to be more sensitive than countryfolk; and the difficulty of securing adequate housing another. The mere fact of dependence upon cash for all the necessities of life enhances the awareness on the part of parents of the burdens of parenthood.

In the welter of circumstances which hasten or retard the reduction of fertility in the developing countries and which affect their economic development, the issue which is perhaps the most important of all has not yet been mentioned – the attitude and effectiveness of the ruling elite. Both the promotion of economic growth and the solution of demographic problems usually requires in modern circumstances the exercise of an effective governmental will. Economic growth and the decline of fertility in western Europe a century ago came about in large part without government intervention. Today this is rare. The extent and minuteness of governmental control of the growth process in Communist countries needs little emphasis, but in other countries it is also great, especially outside the agricultural sector. Governments initiate and finance schemes to build roads, steel mills, irrigation works, electricity stations, and so on. The public sector is under their control in any case and by tax measures and indicative planning investment decisions in private industry also may be heavily influenced.

Government initiative has already played a decisive part in reducing mortality in developing countries to levels little higher than those in the west. Campaigns to eradicate malaria, to overcome tuberculosis, to secure mass vaccination, to establish public health facilities of all types, to provide pure water supplies, and so on, have been vigorously prosecuted. First attempts to give an effective lead to the drive to reduce fertility have been made in several countries. In Korea, Taiwan, Singapore and Hong Kong, family limitation is spreading with varying degrees of active encouragement by the state. Table 6·5 shows that in a number of small

Table 6·5 Developing countries in which there have been large falls in fertility in recent years (crude birth rates per 1,000)[13]

	1960	1961	1962	1963	1964	1965	1966
Hong Kong	36·0	34·3	33·3	32·8	30·1	27·7	24·9
Singapore	38·7	36·5	35·1	34·7	33·2	31·1	29·9
Taiwan	39·5	38·3	37·4	36·3	34·5	32·7	32·5
Trinidad and Tobago	39·1	38·1	38·2	35·6	34·6	28·9	29·4

countries very marked falls in fertility have occurred in recent years. Big states have become committed to the same end. The Indian government provided for family planning expenditure in its First Five-Year Plan in the early 1950s and has increased its expenditure immensely since then. At first results were disappointing, but the advent of the IUD (intra-uterine device) and the contraceptive pill has greatly changed the general outlook and the government now hopes to reduce the crude birth rate from about 40 per 1,000 to about 25 per 1,000 by 1975. In Pakistan, where fertility is even higher than in India, the state was slower to act but is now also strongly committed to a campaign to reduce the birth rate.

No matter how determined a ruling *élite* may be, its power to effect change is, of course, limited by the attitude of the population under its rule. In traditional societies opposition to change, even to trivial changes, is always strong, or perhaps it would be more accurate to say that the ability to accept or understand change is limited. Where authoritarian personality traits are displayed by most men, this restricts what can be done even when a small ruling elite has partially broken free from this constriction. Where, as is

often the case, the ruling elite itself tends to conform to the personality patterns characteristics of the bulk of the population, change
will not come easily, and may be accompanied by much violence.
Does this imply that attempts to spread the knowledge and practice
of contraception made by a government convinced of their importance are foredoomed to frustration?

Reduction of fertility in the developing countries

There is increasing reason to doubt some of the earlier generalisations about the prevalence of social attitudes and institutions
favouring high fertility in traditional societies. It has been claimed,
for example, that one or more of the following points hold good
for most such societies.

First, that a large family was desirable because to some extent a
man's standing depended on the size of his family. This is particularly easy to illustrate from societies in which lineages are important.
For example, in the Ashanti areas studied by Fortes all members of
a lineage feel joy at the birth of any new child to the lineage (in this
case the lineage is matrilineal comprising all those descended from
a common ancestress about ten generations back).[14] High fertility
and low mortality are valued because the influence of individual
members of a lineage depends upon its collective power and
prestige. But even in societies where the conjugal family was of
greater relative importance and the lineage of less, to have many
children might well enhance the standing of a man in his community.
This is indeed, as it were, consonant with reason. In such communities population growth was very slight and the fact that one family
might have five sons who grew to maturity was counterbalanced
by the fact that other families might have no sons who survived
childhood. In the next generation, other things being equal, the
family with many sons would control a larger share of the total
wealth and manpower of the community. The community as a
whole was not necessarily the better off for this, but the individual
family might well be so.

A second consideration reinforces the first and is closely connected to it. Where mortality rates are high and many children die before reaching maturity several sons are needed in order to reduce to negligible levels the risk that there will be no male heir to succeed to the family's land. Moreover, a large family is an insurance policy against discomfort and even outright starvation in the declining years of life.

Thirdly, religious beliefs and sanctions may help to keep fertility high, as, for example, in Catholic Latin America where the church strongly opposes almost all contraceptive practises. High fertility may not be exactly a duty, but taking steps to prevent a conception occurring, or alternatively to prevent it going to term, are almost invariably sinful actions.

In recent years, however, it has become evident that in the developing countries high fertility is not always highly prized. Twenty years ago, for example, a field study in Puerto Rico showed that there most people were prepared to condone contraception for many purposes, and there was a very general belief that the ideal family size was small,[15] with a marked preference for two or three children only, as table 6·6 shows. Since the late 1940s surveys in many Asiatic and South American countries have shown that the average desired family size in developing countries almost always lies in the range 3·0–4·5 (in both Britain and France for comparison the figure is 2·8). It is seldom clear whether respondents to these surveys were discounting infant mortality or not, but in any case the absence of any significant number of respondents holding to the principle 'the bigger, the better' is very notable.

If the surveys and other evidence can be taken at face value, there is a general desire to keep families small in most developing countries. How long this has been true it is impossible to say, but it is easy to show that many of the considerations which once made high fertility so important have lost much of their force. For example, when infant and child mortality rates have fallen to low levels there is no point in having a large family to guard against a failure of the male line or a childless old age. Indeed, the boot is on the

Table 6·6 Puerto Rican adults' views on ideal family size (1947); figures in percentages[16]

Ideal family size	Men	Women	Ideal family size	Men	Women
0	0·3	0·1	5	4·7	3·8
1	2·2	2·4	6–8	4·2	3·2
2	45·7	50·5	9 plus	1·0	0·6
3	27·0	26·7	As God wills	2·3	1·9
4	12·5	10·9			

Note From a small number of households (about two per cent) no answer was obtained; they are excluded from the percentage figures.

other foot. Now the problem of finding dowries or avoiding the division of holdings may loom large and the danger of dying without successors recedes into the background.

Other obstacles to reduced fertility may weaken also. Different elements in religious traditions may be emphasised which do not stress the importance of high fertility. Again, increasing urbanisation, in undermining the extended family system, may change both the habitual age at first marriage for women and bring a clearer recognition of the advantages of the small family.

It is too early to be dogmatic about the speed with which fertility rates in the developing countries may change, and it would be rash to assume that all will change with equal swiftness, or even in the same direction. Social disruption may increase as well as lower fertility. Nevertheless, since the normal drift of argument until recently has been to doubt the possibility of swift or substantial falls in fertility, it is well to recall those points which suggest the opposite.

In the first place fertility rates in many traditional societies were not notably high. Sometimes social customs governing behaviour within marriage had the effect of keeping fertility low. Sometimes low fertility was the result of deliberate action. Sometimes, as among the Baganda, an unusually high percentage of women were childless (24 per cent of women of completed fertility in the 1948 census).[17] Whatever the reason, however, the wide range of marital fertility levels observable in pre-industrial societies suggests that in many developing countries today there are elements of customary practice which are linked to fertility control, though this may seldom be consciously recognised. Where these circumstances exist societies may respond the more readily to attempts to reduce fertility further.

Secondly, the new methods of contraception are important in their own right. This is especially true of the IUD which appears to meet most of the prime prerequisites of a contraceptive for the developing countries. It is very cheap. Once successfully fitted it requires no further attention, and it does not make it necessary for couples to turn love-making into a premeditated act. Moreover, it is reasonably reliable. Field trials in Taiwan, for example, suggest a failure rate of about five pregnancies per 100 woman-years. From the point of view of achieving a big fall in fertility this is perfectly adequate. It is true that between five and ten per cent of women fitted with the IUD reject it naturally. Sometimes a second fitting is then successful. A further group, about an eighth of the total number, had the device removed because they suffered side effects.[18] Even so the fall in fertility over a society as a whole may easily be enough to reduce population growth substantially over a decade or two. Old contraceptive methods are much more expensive and experience has shown that they are rarely adopted on a wide scale except among fairly well educated groups. The best of contraceptives is useless unless it is in position, and in the days before the IUD or the pill, contraceptive devices had to be separately fitted for each occasion. This helps to explain the long continued popularity of *coitus interruptus* which enjoys the further advantage of costing nothing.

Thirdly, there have already been large falls in fertility in several developing countries in recent years (see table 6·5). Places like Hong Kong and Singapore are not, of course, typical of the vast mass of rural, peasant society. But in these cities the fall in birth rates has been abrupt and rapid. It may presage slower falls in rural areas, and indeed the changes in Taiwan show that populations composed largely of peasants may follow a similar path.

It would be premature to assume that the changes now visible in Taiwan or Singapore will be paralleled throughout the high fertility areas. Some countries in which a fall in the birth rate might be expected to have occurred by now show an unwaveringly high fertility. For example, the Mexican crude birth rate has been constant in the range of 45–47 per 1,000 for many years in spite of Mexico's close proximity to the United States. On the other hand, there are countries other than those of western Europe or of European settlement overseas in which fertility has now fallen to very low levels. In Japan, for example, the gross reproduction rate is now below unity. Nor is Japan the only area outside western Europe where such a change has taken place, for in eastern Europe the last two generations have seen great changes similar to those which have taken place in Japan, and eastern Europe three-quarters of a century ago had much in common with the developing countries today. In eastern Europe, for example, marriage in the late teens was normal for girls and few remained unmarried at 20 (see table 6·7). Fertility was very high with crude birth rates above 40 per 1,000. In some parts of eastern Europe the extended family system still prevailed, and economically also eastern Europe resembled the developing world today while standing in marked contrast with western Europe. The great bulk of the labour force in countries like Bulgaria and Rumania worked on the land and in subsistence rather than commercial agriculture. Much of south-eastern Europe indeed had only recently ceased to be a colonial area subject to Turkish rule. Yet some of the lowest fertility rates anywhere in the

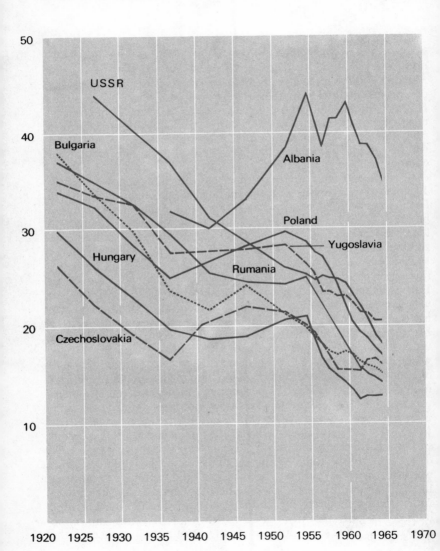

Figure 6·3 Falling crude birth rates in eastern European Countries (per 1000 total population).[19]

Table 6·7 Percentages of women never married in three age-groups and at various dates[20]

		Date	20–4	25–9	45–9
Eastern Europe	Rumania	1899	20	8	3
	Bulgaria	1900	24	3	1
	Serbia	1900	16	2	1
Africa and Asia	Egypt	1947	20	6	1
	Mauritius	1952	24	12	5
	Taiwan	1930	15	4	0
	Ceylon	1946	29	12	3
Western Europe	Great Britain	1901	73	42	15
	France	1901	58	30	12
	Germany	1900	71	34	10

world are found today in Hungary and Rumania, and all over eastern Europe fertility fell greatly both between the wars and again in the last decade (see figure 6·3). Abortion was very widely practised in eastern Europe (as in Japan).[21] Abortion rates are reported to have reached astonishing levels in some cities. In Moscow in 1934, for example, the rate is said to have been 2·71 abortions for every live birth.[22] A Hungarian inquiry carried out in 1958–60 revealed that about two-thirds of all married women 30–44 had had recourse to abortion to prevent births, and as many as 29 per cent of those in the age-group 15–19 had done so.[23] In 1963 there were 131 legal abortions performed for every 100 live births in Hungary.[24]

In recent years (again as in Japan) most eastern European countries have made a legal abortion very much easier to obtain with the results to be seen in figure 6·3. Between 1956 and 1961 legislation to this effect occurred in Russia, Poland, Hungary, Bulgaria, Czechoslovakia, Rumania and Yugoslavia. The gross reproduction rate was close to unity in all countries of eastern Europe by the early 1960s (except for Albania, Chinese in this as in other matters) and below unity in Hungary and Rumania.

Coale recently laid his head upon the block and predicted that by 1970 fertility would have fallen by at least 25 per cent in Korea and China; by 1975 in India and Pakistan; and by 1980 in much of Latin America.[25] Fertility predictions usually do more honour to an author's reputation for courage than for accuracy, and events may well prove Coale wrong, but large and rapid fertility declines in the developing countries are clearly possible. Demographers have consistently underestimated the speed of the fall of death rates in the last 20 years; they may well tend to err in the same way over birth rates in the next 20 years.

The population problems of wealthy countries

At first sight it seems odd to write of population problems in the rich countries. We are so frequently reminded of the disasters threatening the poorer countries because of the press of population within their borders that it requires an effort of the imagination to understand that the rich countries also have their problems. In western Europe, North America and Australasia (and indeed in Russia and Japan too) a growing population and a rising standard of living have long ceased to be conflicting alternatives. Both can be secured simultaneously. If population is rising by, say, one per cent per annum and real income per head by two per cent, then in terms of the traditional Malthusian dilemma the circle has been squared: there is no problem.

Figure 6.4 Three projections of the population of England and Wales (in millions).[26]

A fertility and mortality as in 1933

B continued fall in fertility and mortality in conformity with inter-war experience

C actual course of population to 1965: then Registrar-General's projection of 1962

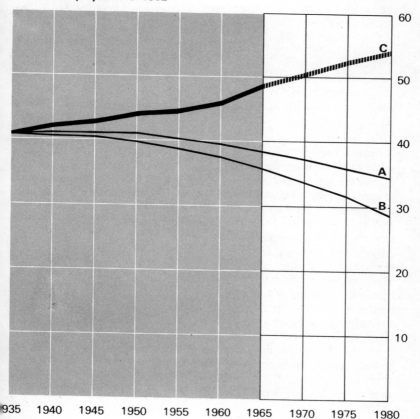

Table 6·8 Inter-war reproduction rates in some west European countries[27]

	1925		1930		1935		1939	
	GRR	NRR	GRR	NRR	GRR	NRR	GRR	NRR
Denmark			1.069*	0.949*	1.029	0.922	1.041	0.940
France	1.160	0.940	1.110	0.930	1.000	0.870	1.060	0.930
Germany			0.862*	0.748*	1.037	0.906		
Norway			1.036†	0.890†	0.869	0.746	0.932	0.849
Sweden	1.121	1.018	0.966	0.878	0.812	0.739	0.910	0.830
United Kingdom	1.074	0.928	0.953	0.840	0.854	0.764	0.892	0.808

*1931   †1930–1

Note GRR = gross reproduction rate, NRR = net reproduction rate

In order to grasp the sense in which the wealthy countries today may be said to have population problems, it is helpful to outline their recent demographic history. The fall in fertility in these countries brought about by the spread of contraception had gone very far by the inter-war years. In several countries net reproduction rates were well below unity and even gross reproduction rates were in some instances below this level (table 6·8). In general it is true both that the fall in fertility had gone furthest in the wealthiest countries and that within each country the richest groups had the lowest fertility. It was therefore sometimes argued that the inverse correlation between fertility and wealth could be raised to the dignity of a demographic law. This situation caused widespread alarm. A steady decline in population seemed inevitable in many countries. Figure 6·4 shows two projections made by Charles in the mid 1930s. In projection **A** she assumed that fertility and mortality in England and Wales would remain at their 1933 level: in **B** that both would continue to decline. The two curves represent the upper and lower limits of what she thought it reasonable to expect. Projection **C** shows how far events have moved away from the paths she felt it worthwhile to explore. Much the same is true of the several projections made by Thompson and Whelpton for the United States and of dozens of similar exercises carried out in the late 1930s.[28]

Both the generalisations of the 1930s about the inverse relationships between wealth and fertility have been falsified by the course of history. Fertility is no longer lowest in the richest countries; nor is it always lower in the richer groups in a population than the poorer (see pages 186–9). There has been a general recovery in fertility assisted by some further falls in infant and child mortality. As a result reproduction rates are well above unity in most wealthy countries, with rates of population increase usually between one half and one-and-a-half per cent per annum.

The change has come about both because marital fertility has risen and because fewer and fewer women remain single. Table 5·17 (page 197) shows in summary form how marital fertility has changed in England. Mean completed family size has grown considerably from its lowest point of 2·04 in the marriage cohort of 1950–4. This change alone, of course, must raise fertility, but the effect has been compounded by the marked tendency for fewer women to remain spinsters (table 6·9). A far higher proportion of women were married in the 30–4 age group in 1961 than even in the 45–9 age group in, say, 1921. Indeed the figure was higher than that for the 45–9 age group in 1961 itself. During the period of rapidly declining marital fertility in the late nineteenth century in England the proportion of women who never married rose, thus accentuating the fall in general fertility. Since 1921 the proportion has fallen and since 1941 has fallen very markedly. Broadly similar changes have occurred in the last generation in many western countries. Since the 1930s also age at first marriage has fallen for both sexes, in England and Wales (table 6·10), coinciding with the rising proportions ever married (a tendency for age at first marriage to vary inversely with proportions ever married has been observed in many populations).

Population growth as a problem in a wealthy country

As a result of the changes just described there is no longer any clear-cut relationship between real incomes per head and fertility levels among the more economically advanced countries (table 6·11). Crude birth rates are not a perfect guide to fertility but it is interesting to see the lowest rates in Sweden and Hungary, the one very wealthy, the other comparatively poor. If it is not true that the converse of the position believed typical in the 1930s has been reached, it is certainly true that no simple pattern yet emerges.

The decay of the once widespread inverse correlation between wealth and fertility rates both within industrialised countries and between them may seem a healthy development. If nowadays it is increasingly the case that those families and countries best able to afford more children have regained rather higher fertility levels, while among the less wealthy fertility has fallen, surely this is to be welcomed?

In economic terms the answer to this question must clearly be 'yes', but the very absence of opposition between rising population and rising real incomes brings with it problems of a different sort. How far can numbers rise before penalties of a non-economic type are paid? If there are complaints about overcrowding and lack of privacy, about the destruction of the countryside and the spread of suburbs, in an England of 45 million people living on 32 million acres, how much worse will these problems become if numbers rise to 100 millions, 200 millions, even 500 millions? It is entirely possible that sufficient wealth can be produced to support even a population ten times the present size in greater material comfort than is enjoyed today. Material technology progresses swiftly and no bar to further progress of this sort is immediately in sight. Even the bottleneck of food supply from a static or declining acreage of farm land may be eased by the discovery of ways of synthesising foods in short supply. But is the prospect of a decupling of population tolerable on other grounds?

In England today there are about two acres available for each

Table 6·9 Proportions of men and women ever married in England and Wales 1881–1961 (per 1,000)[29]

	Men				Women			
	30–4	35–9	40–4	45–9	30–4	35–9	40–4	45–9
1881	769	848	878	901	777	834	861	877
1901	748	824	861	886	745	801	831	858
1921	769	837	863	876	740	796	821	832
1941	803	864	888	906	783	810	827	831
1951	819	867	892	902	855	869	860	848
1961	845	882	893	910	909	911	912	896

Table 6·10 Mean age at first marriage in England and Wales (in years)[30]

	Men	Women		Men	Women
1911–15	27·49	25·75	1951–5	26·55	24·18
1921–5	27·47	25·57	1960	25·68	23·26
1936–40	27·51	25·38	1964	25·24	22·78

Table 6·11 Average crude birth rates 1960–4 in Europe (per 1,000 total population)[31]

Hungary	13·6	France	18·0	Italy	18·9
Sweden	14·5	Finland	18·1	Poland	20·0
Czechoslovakia	16·3	United Kingdom	18·2	Netherlands	20·9
Bulgaria	16·9	West Germany	18·3	Spain	21·6

family. In most other countries the figure is much larger; in a few it is even less. But the problem remains in principle the same for all countries. If the number of families in England were to increase ten times, then the area available on average for each family would shrink to just over 30 yards square. Upon this land not only would all housing needs have to be met, but room found for factories, roads, airfields, all farming activities, government offices, shops, parks, all sporting facilities, and so on. The prospect of having to wrestle with space allocation problems in this situation is not an immediate one, but the population of England would rise to ten times its present size in about 470 years at a rate of increase as low as one half per cent per annum. The problem cannot, therefore, be said to be comfortably remote. Even a simple doubling of the population, which might happen within the next two or three generations, would certainly entail serious problems of space planning.

When a man achieves a higher income he often decides to move to a larger house with a bigger garden. His growing wealth also finds expression in a growing demand for golf courses, tennis courts, swimming pools, football pitches; for opportunities to ride, walk, climb, ski; for more motorways, parking areas, service stations, and so on. In the main the wealthier the man the more of these things he will want. By encroaching on the countryside these needs can be met even in densely populated countries for some time yet. But the open countryside slowly shrinks and the many intangible benefits which spring from the existence of large areas of wild or agricultural land are lost. While, therefore, it may become easier and easier to produce all manner of industrial goods, and even possibly food if most foods can be synthesised on a factory scale, those things on which much wealth is spent, those things which make wealth, as it were, worthwhile, will be in shorter and shorter supply. There exists, or may exist, a conflict between the general and the particular interests of men.

Conflict of private and public interest

If, in a community whose wealth is growing, the marginal satisfaction derived by a couple from enlarging their family is greater than that which can be had from acquiring a second car or moving to a more expensive house, they will welcome a new child. If many families share the same sentiments the fertility of the whole community will rise. The same will happen if, even without a general rise in living standards, there are changes in attitude to family size (for example, a growing feeling against a one-child family in the belief that it is good for a child to have brothers and sisters).

The creation of new life is a wonderful and rewarding experience in itself for many parents. In the wealthier countries the financial penalties paid for a large family are less severe than was once the case, especially where there are family allowances or where the tax structure reduces the net cost of adding to a family by relieving it of part of the tax burden to which it would otherwise be liable. Many husbands and wives may come to feel that it is important to their happiness that their families should be, if not large, then at least more frequently in the 3–5 range than in the 0–2 range. Even a slight shift in preferences in this direction may increase the rate of population growth markedly.

Yet those same couples who in their private capacity want to have relatively large families may find that the amenities which they wish to have for themselves and their children are increasingly difficult to obtain if others also have larger families. The additional pressure upon amenities caused by any one large family is, of course, trivial, but if many families are larger the change is appreciable even in the short run. In the longer term, as the operation of geometrical progression adds larger and larger absolute numbers to the population in each succeeding year, the change grows drastically great. Collectively, the interest of all couples jointly will lie in stability of numbers or very modest increase.

It is as yet premature to assume that this problem will materialise. Movements of fertility have proved difficult to predict in the past

Table 6·12 Recent falls in crude birth rates in North America and Australasia (per 1,000 total population)[32]

	1940—4	1945—9	1950—4	1955—9
Australia	19·5	23·1	23·0	22·6
Canada	23·2	27·0	27·7	27·8
New Zealand	22·8	26·5	25·8	26·3
United States	19·9	23·4	24·6	24·7

and present trends may well alter. A modest fall in fertility would ensure that the next generation is no larger than the present in most industrialised countries, and there have recently been signs that such a fall is now taking place. Table 6·12 shows, for example, that crude birth rates have fallen quite sharply in the English-speaking countries outside Europe and reproduction rates have also sagged in parallel. Nevertheless it is important that the problem should have a full hearing, bearing it in mind that if rising numbers do produce a notable deterioration in the amenities of life, the worsening trend can only be reversed if either mortality rises (which is both unlikely and unacceptable as a solution) or fertility falls for a time so low that successive generations grow smaller and average family size sinks to two or less. This would be to penalise later generations. Control exercised at an early stage is much to be preferred to any more drastic adjustment either of fertility or mortality later on. The act of bringing a child into the world, though so essentially a matter which concerns one mother and one father above all others, is nevertheless also an act which intimately concerns society as a whole.

In order to produce a rough stability of population in the long

1960	1961	1962	1963	1964	1965	1966
22·4	22·8	22·1	21·6	20·6	19·6	19·3
26·7	26·0	25·3	24·6	23·5	21·4	19·6
26·5	27·1	26·2	25·5	24·1	22·8	22·5
23·7	23·3	22·4	21·7	21·0	19·4	18·5

term, mean family size in industrialised countries would usually have to be reduced by about a quarter or half a child, or, to put the matter rather less perversely, it would be necessary to induce every 100 married couples to have 25 to 50 fewer children *in toto*. This is a very modest change. It might well be secured by the abolition of children's allowances in those countries in which they are paid. In other countries, or wherever their abolition proved insufficient, it would be well to consider tapering off tax reliefs for successive children, or in extreme cases increasing the tax commitments of a man who increased his family beyond a certain point.

The basic problem remains simple. Different men may well judge differently how dense a population is tolerable and a consensus of opinion may as yet be hard to obtain, but almost all men would agree that numbers could reach such a level that all would suffer as a result. Any density, however great, will be reached in time if populations continue to grow. At some point, therefore, all men would be agreed in hoping to see further increase cease. And at that point men and women must accustom themselves to the small family (an average of about two-and-a-quarter children). The difficulties involved in reaching such a state of balance between fertility and mortality cannot be avoided: they can only be postponed.

The matter cannot be left to take care of itself, as was once possible. The days when rising population pressure tended to increase death rates and so to arrest population growth are over. The evolution of a new code of social discipline influencing family formation is necessary. It may possibly arise without public debate or state action as one of those mysterious adjustments to changing circumstances which societies make from time to time. But it seems more likely that the problem can be met only by society evolving a new consensus about the principles on which limits to population growth might be defined and the means judged appropriate to secure a reduction in fertility as the limits are approached.

It was said (by a Russian) in the early days of American space rocketry that they had solved all the miniaturisation problems involved in enabling comparatively small rockets to lift useful payloads into space except that of miniaturising men. We shall face a similar problem in the industrialised, wealthy countries if the fertility levels of the 1950s and early 1960s are maintained for several more generations. Beyond a certain point the quality of people's lives will suffer because of their number. Quality of life and quantity of men are in opposition.

In medieval times a man felt in his belly the penalties of over-large population. Today he may not feel it in his belly or even in his pocket, yet his impoverishment is real, if men are not rabbits to live in hutches. 'Soon London', James I remarked early in the seventeenth century, 'will be all England'. Even Dr Johnson, for all his advocacy of life there, might blench at what is now much more than a figure of speech. If men are to have the space necessary to take advantage of their newly acquired wealth, cities and their facilities must cover larger and larger areas per citizen. This sets a limit to the number of citizens whose needs can be met. The industrialised countries, therefore, face population problems because of their wealth as teasing, if less immediately terrible, as those which haunt the developing countries because of their poverty.

References here are given in brief. Full details of each book or article are to be found in the bibliography. The bibliography also contains details of the abbreviations of journal titles.

1 Historical demography

1. The passage occurs in *Ideas for a universal history of mankind*. See Rabel, *Kant*, 134.
2. Based on United Nations, *Methods for population projections by sex and age*, 72–3, tab. 1.
3. *Report from Mr. Finlaison*, Parl. Papers, 1829, III, 297.
4. Goode, *World revolution and family patterns*, 207–11.
5. *Census of Ireland 1901*, Parl. Papers 1902, CXXIX, pt. II, 395, tab. 87.
6. United Nations, *Demographic Yearbook*, 1963, tab. 34.
7. United Nations, *Demographic Yearbook*, 1961, tab. 26.
8. Eaton and Mayer, *Hum. Biol.* (1953), 225 and 231.
9. Bourgeois-Pichat, *Pop.* (1965), 401, tab. 7.
10. United Nations, *Demographic Yearbook*, 1964, tab. 5.
11. Coale and Hoover, *Population growth and economic development*, 235, tab. 32.
12. Coale, *Milbank Mem. Fund Qu.* (1956); and United Nations, *The aging of populations*, esp. chap. 2.
13. United Nations, *The aging of populations*, 26, tab. 15.

2 The size of populations

1. Smith, *Wealth of nations*, 169.
2. Malthus, *First essay on population*, 130.
3. Malthus, *First essay on population*, 131. See also Boulding, *Soc. & Ec. Stud.* (1955).
4. Darwin, in *Charles Darwin and Alfred Russel Wallace*, 118.
5. Darwin, in *Charles Darwin and Alfred Russel Wallace*, 117.
6. Darwin, *On the origin of species*, 75.
7. Wynne-Edwards, *Animal dispersion*, 10 and 560; **Watt.** *Can. Entom.* (1960).
8. Wynne-Edwards, *Animal dispersion*, 10.
9. Wynne-Edwards, *Animal dispersion*, 139, 150, 531 and 566–9.
10. Wynne-Edwards, *Animal dispersion*, 512.

11. Himes, *Medical history of contraception*, 18.
12. Lorimer, in *Culture and human fertility*, 107 and 390.
13. Himes, *Medical history of contraception*, 51–2.
14. Himes, *Medical history of contraception*, 39.
15. Carr-Saunders, *The population problem*, 161.
16. Krzywicki, *Primitive society*, 130.
17. Carr-Saunders, *The population problem*, 216–8.
18. Lorimer, in *Culture and human fertility*, 131; Krzywicki, *Primitive society*, 192–3.
19. Douglas, *Br. J. Sociol* (1966), 268. See also Carr-Saunders, *The population problem*, 147–8.
20. Carr-Saunders, *The population problem*, 160.
21. Lorimer, in *Culture and human fertility*, 105–9.
22. Douglas, *Br. J. Sociol.* (1966), 269–70.
23. Krzywicki, *Primitive society*, 125.
24. Krzywicki, *Primitive society*, 182.
25. Carr-Saunders, *The population problem*, 217.
26. Clark and Haswell, *The economics of subsistence agriculture*, 25–7.
27. Boserup, *The conditions of agricultural growth*, 57.
28. John, in *Essays in economic history*, 373.
29. This is a main theme of Boserup, *The conditions of agricultural growth*.
30. Malthus, *First essay on population*, 137–8.
31. Mitchell and Deane, *British historical statistics*, 6.
32. Keynes, *The economic consequences of the Peace* 7–8 and 20–2; and *Ec. J.* (1923).
33. Wrigley, *Ec. Hist. Rev.* (1962), esp. 1–6.
34. Benaerts, *Les origines de la grande industrie allemande*, 454.
35. *Agricultural Statistics 1963/4*, 53, tab. 52.
36. Deane and Cole, *British economic growth*, 67; conversion factor used, 1·81 bushels of wheat = 1 cwt.
37. Godwin, *Of population*, 500–1.

3 Fluctuations in pre-industrial populations

1. Lassen, *Scand. Ec. Hist. Rev.* (1965), 29.
2. Jutikkala, *Scand. Ec. Hist. Rev.* (1955).
3. George, *London life in the eighteenth century*, 171.
4. Goubert, *Annales* (1952), 468.

5. Drake, *Scand. Ec. Hist. Rev.* (1965), 124.
6. Goubert, *Annales* (1952), 466.
7. Goubert, *Beauvais et le Beauvaisis*, II, 56–7. Professor Goubert was kind enough to supplement by letter the details to be found on these pages.
8. Goubert, *Beauvais et la Beauvaisis*, I, 404.
9. Drake, *Scand. Ec. Hist. Rev.* (1965), 110, tab. 4.
10. Mitchell and Deane, *British historical statistics*, 485.
11. Utterström, *Scand. Ec. Hist. Rev.* (1954). See also Gille, *Pop. Stud.* (1949), esp. 50–4.
12. A characteristic passage may be found in Tooke, *History of prices*, I, 62–85.
13. Razzell, *Ec. Hist. Rev.* (1965).
14. See, for example, Goubert, in *Problèmes de mortalité*, 88; and Ruwet, in *Problèmes de mortalité*, 398–403.
15. Fleury and Henry, *Nouveau manuel*. See also Wrigley (ed.), *English historical demography*; and Krause, *Comp. Stud. Soc. & Hist.* (1959).
16. Wrigley, *Ec. Hist. Rev.* (1966), 84, fig. 1.
17. Levy, in *Analysis of family structure*, 26–7.
18. Wrigley, *Ec. Hist. Rev.* (1966), esp. 100–5; for mortality, Wrigley, *Daedalus* (1968).
19. Hajnal, in *Population in history*.
20. Herlihy, *Ec. Hist. Rev.* (1965), 235–7.
21. Gautier and Henry, *La population de Crulai*, 102 and 105; Wrigley, *Ec. Hist. Rev.* (1966), 89, tab. 4; Rele, *Pop. Stud.* (1962), 269, tab. 2; Lorimer, in *Culture and human fertility*, 26–7, tab. 1.
22. Rele, *Pop. Stud.* (1962), 272.
23. On this general issue see Bourgeois-Pichat, *Pop.* (1965), and Potter, *Pop. Stud.* (1963).
24. Henripin, *La population canadienne*, 66, tab. xvIIIb; Deprez, in *Population in history*, 618; Eaton and Mayer, *Hum. Biol.* (1953), 230, tab. 13.
25. Farr, *Vital statistics*, 165.
26. Pullan, *Boll. Ist. Stor. Soc.* (1963–4).
27. Creighton, *History of epidemics*, I, 660.
28. Wrigley, *P. & P.* (1967).
29. Sjoberg, *The preindustrial city*.
30. Mols, *La démographie des villes d'Europe*, II, chap. 11.
31. Short, *New observations*, 68.
32. I owe this information to the courtesy of Mr F. West who acquainted

me with the results of his researches into the history of Wrangle.
33. Drake, *Marriage and population growth in Norway*, 97–101 and 157–8, tab. 53, 54, 55 and 56.
34. Derived from Hollingsworth, *Pop. Stud.* (1964), 15, tab. 6.
35. Goode, *World revolution and family patterns*, 286–7.
36. Wrigley, *Ec. Hist. Rev.* (1966), 88.

4 Society and economy in pre-industrial populations

1. Wynne-Edwards, *Animal dispersion*, 9.
2. Graunt, in *The economic writings of Sir William Petty*, II, 408.
3. Goode, *World revolution and family patterns*, 124.
4. Laslett, *The world we have lost*, 90–1.
5. Gautier and Henry, *La population de Crulai*, 67.
6. Henry, *Anciennes familles genevoises*.
7. Henry, *Anciennes familles genevoises*, 76.
8. Petersen, *Population*, 2–3.
9. Henry, *Anciennes familles genevoises*, 94.
10. Henry, *Anciennes familles genevoises*, 100.
11. Henry, *Anciennes familles genevoises*, 89.
12. Banks, *Prosperity and parenthood*.
13. Deniel and Henry, *Pop.* (1965), 575; Valmary, *Familles paysannes en Bas-Quercy*, 120.
14. Wrigley, *Ec. Hist. Rev.* (1966), 89, tab. 4.
15. Calculated from data in Deniel and Henry, *Pop.* (1965), 572; and Valmary, *Familles paysannes en Bas-Quercy*, 101.
16. Gautier and Henry, *La population de Crulai*, 151.
17. Bergues and others, *La prévention des naissances dans la famille*.
18. Helleiner, *J. Ec. Hist.* (1958), 60–1.
19. Wrigley, *Ec. Hist. Rev.* (1966), esp. 104–5.
20. Petersen, *Population*, 547.
21. Burn, *The ecclesiastical law*, II, 513.
22. Burn, *The ecclesiastical law*, II, 513.
23. Bergues, in *La prévention des naissances dans la famille*, 173–4 and 180–5.
24. Stone, *P. & P.* (1966), 42.
25. Wilson, *England's apprenticeship*, 352. See George, *London life in the eighteenth century*, 409, however, for details of Hanway's work which suggest a lower figure, perhaps about 65 per cent *c.* 1765.

26. I am indebted for information about this case to the Rev. R. A. Marchant and Mr R. C. Richardson. The record is to be found in the Borthwick Institute of Historical Research at York, R.vi.A.12, ff. 78–9.
27. Creighton, *History of epidemics*, i, 495.
28. Creighton, *History of epidemics*, i, 491–2.
29. Creighton, *History of epidemics*, i, 317.
30. Pressat, *L'analyse démographique*, 116.
31. Gautier and Henry, *La population de Crulai*, 192.
32. Calculated with the aid of specimen life tables from data in Demos, *W. & M. Qu.* (1965), 271.
33. United Nations, *Methods for population projections by sex and age*, 76, tab. iii.
34. Levy and Westoff, *New Scientist* (1965).
35. Ohlin, *Pop. Stud.* (1961).
36. Slicher van Bath, *Agrarian history of western Europe*, 314.
37. Deprez, in *Population in history*, esp. 628.
38. Deprez, in *Population in history*, 620.
39. Wrigley, *Industrial growth and population change*, 9–10.
40. Habakkuk, in *The family*, 167.
41. Thirsk, in *Essays in the economic and social history of Tudor and Stuart England*.
42. Leibenstein, *Economic backwardness and economic growth*, 127.
43. This is a main theme, for example, of Goode, *World revolution and family patterns*.

5 Population and the industrial revolution

1. Wrigley, *P. & P.* (1967).
2. Reinhard and Armengaud, *Histoire générale de la population mondiale*, 166, 173, 175, 179 and 200; Deane and Cole, *British economic growth*, 6, tab. 2.
3. *Statistik des Deutschen Reichs*, Erste Reihe, xxxvii (Juli), Übersicht i, 'Bevölkerung der Deutschen Staaten und ihrer grösseren Verwaltungs-bezirke in der Begrenzung zur Zeit der jedesmaligen Volkszählung seit 1816'.
4. Drake, *Scand. Ec. Hist. Rev.* (1965), 108, tab. 2 and 130, tab. i.
5. Wrigley, *Industrial growth and population change*, 144, tab. 40.
6. Wrigley, *Industrial growth and population change*, 133, tab. 34 and 141, tab. 39.

240

7. Wrigley, *Industrial growth and population change*, 143–5, tab. 40.
8. Drake, *Scand. Ec. Hist. Rev.* (1965), 136, tab. VII
9. Goode, *World revolution and family patterns*, 51–2.
10. Registrar-General, *Statistical Review for 1933*, pt. 1, 6, tab. 5; and *Statistical Review for 1962*, pt. 1, 6, tab. 4. Approximations for the age group 1–4 were made using material from several censuses. See also McKeown and Record, *Pop. Stud.* (1962).
11. United Nations, *Determinants and consequences of population trends*, 54, tab. 5.
12. Wrigley, *Industrial growth and population change*, 101, tab. 24.
13. Ensor, *England 1870–1914*, 35 and 127.
14. Drummond and Wilbraham, *The Englishman's food*, 404.
15. Rowntree, *Poverty*, 112, 117 and 206.
16. Farr, *Vital statistics*, 466, 477 and 478.
17. Weber, *The growth of cities*, 349.
18. Wrigley, *Industrial growth and population change*, 99, tab. 23.
19. Wrigley, *Industrial growth and population change*, 122, tab. 31.
20. *Pop.* (1964), 973.
21. Creighton, *History of epidemics*, I, 171.
22. Solow, *Rev. Ec. & Stat.* (1957), 320.
23. Deane and Cole, *British economic growth*, 143.
24. Wrigley, *Industrial growth and population change*, 133, tab. 34 and 141, tab. 39.
25. Reinhard and Armengaud, *Histoire générale de la population mondiale*, 226: Deane and Cole, *British economic growth*, 8, tab. 3.
26. *Royal Commission on Population*, VI, pt. 1, 110, tab. 40.
27. Wrigley, *Industrial growth and population change*, 133, tab. 34; 141, tab. 39 and 142, tab. 40.
28. *Census 1961*, Fertility Tables, tab. 14.
29. *Royal Commission on Population*, I, 8, tab. 5.
30. Levasseur, *La population française*, III, 171–7.
31. Banks, *Prosperity and parenthood*, esp. chap. 12.
32. Registrar-General, *Statistical Review for 1963*, pt. III, 64, tab. C36.
33. Registrar-General, *Statistical Review for 1963*, pt. III, 67, tab. C40
34. Registrar-General, *Statistical Review for 1961*, pt. III, 70, tab. XLII; and *Statistical Review for 1963*, pt. III, 75, tab. C44.
35. *Royal Commission on Population*, VI, pt. I, 87, tab. 16.
36. Registrar-General, *Statistical Review for 1962*, pt. I, tab. 13.

37. Pressat, *L'analyse démographique*, 345.
38. United Nations, *Demographic Yearbook*, 1963, tab. 26.

6 For richer, for poorer

1. United Nations, *Demographic Yearbook*, 1963, tab. 26.
2. Durand, *Proc. Am. Phil. Soc.* (1967), 137, tab. 1.
3. Coale and Hoover, *Population growth and economic development*, 35, tab. 3; 36, tab. 4 and 38, tab. 6.
4. Beckerman and Bacon, *Ec. J.* (1966), 533, tab. VI.
5. United Nations, *Demographic Yearbook*, 1957, tab. 8; 1961, tab. 14 and 1965, tab. 12 and 14.
6. Boserup, *The conditions of agricultural growth*, 118.
7. Coale and Hoover, *Population growth and economic development*, 273, tab. 38 and 275.
8. Leibenstein, *Economic backwardness and economic growth*, 127-8.
9. Coale and Hoover, *Population growth and economic development*, 248.
10. Coale and Hoover, *Population growth and economic development*, 48.
11. Hatt, *Human fertility in Puerto Rico*, 143, 185 and 249.
12. Coale and Hoover, *Population growth and economic development* 47-8; Robinson, *Pop. Stud.* (1961).
13. United Nations, *Monthly Bulletin of Statistics*, XX, no. 6 (1966) and XXI, no. 8 (1967).
14. Fortes, in *Culture and human fertility*, 266-7 and 270.
15. Hatt, *Human fertility in Puerto Rico*, 79-86.
16. Hatt, *Human fertility in Puerto Rico*, 53, tab. 37.
17. Lorimer, in *Culture and human fertility*, 125. See also 400, tab. 88.
18. Chow, *Pop. Stud.* (1965), 164.
19. United Nations, *Demographic Yearbook*, 1965, tab. 12. See also Szabady and others, *Pop.* (1966).
20. Hajnal, in *Population in history*, 102, tab. 2; 103, tab. 3 and 104, tab. 4.
21. For Japan see Taeuber. *The changing population of Japan*; Taeuber, *Pop. Stud.* (1960); Muramatsu, in *Family planning and population programs*.
22. Petersen, *Population*, 427.
23. *Pop.* (1965), 128.
24. Blayo, *Pop.* (1966), 992.
25. Coale, *Proc. Am. Phil. Soc.* (1967), 169.

26. Charles, in *Political arithmetic*, 82, tab. II and III; and Registrar-General, *Statistical Review for 1962*, pt. II, 2, tab. A1 and 7, tab. A5.
27. United Nations, *Demographic Yearbook*, 1948, tab. 31.
28. Petersen, *Population*, 280–4.
29. Registrar-General, *Statistical Review for 1962*, p. III, 14, tab. XIII.
30. Registrar-General, *Statistical Review for 1964*, pt. II, 60, tab. L.
31. United Nations, *Demographic Yearbook*, 1965, tab. 12.
32. United Nations, *Monthly Bulletin of Statistics*, XXI, no. 8 (1967) and United Nations, *Demographic Yearbook*, 1965, tab. 12.

Bibliography

The books and articles in this list are chiefly those referred to in the endnotes. The titles and other details are here given in full. A few other works of general interest have been added. The most widely useful books and articles are marked with an asterisk.

The following abbreviations of the titles of journals are used:

Bollettino dell'Istituto di Storia della Società e dello Stato	Boll. Ist. Stor. Soc.
British Journal of Sociology	Br. J. Sociol.
Canadian Entomologist	Can. Entom.
Comparative Studies in Society and History	Comp. Stud. Soc. & Hist.
Economic Development and Cultural Change	Ec. Dev. & Cult. Change
Economic History Review	Ec. Hist. Rev.
Economic Journal	Ec. J.
Human Biology	Hum. Biol.
Journal of Economic History	J. Ec. Hist.
Milbank Memorial Fund Quarterly	Milbank Mem. Fund. Qu.
Parliamentary Papers	Parl. Papers
Past and Present	P. & P.
Population	Pop.
Population Studies	Pop. Stud.
Proceedings of the American Philosophical Society	Proc. Am. Phil. Soc.
Review of Economics and Statistics	Rev. Ec. & Stat.
Scandinavian Economic History Review	Scand. Ec. Hist. Rev.
Social and Economic Studies	Soc. & Ec. Stud.
William and Mary Quarterly	W. & M. Qu.

Agricultural Statistics 1963/4, England and Wales (H.M.S.O. 1966).

Ariès, P., *Centuries of childhood* (London, 1963).

Banks, J.A., *Prosperity and parenthood* (London, 1954).

Beckerman, W. and Bacon, E., 'International comparisons of income levels: a suggested measure', *Ec. J.*, LXXVI (1966), 519–36.

Benaerts, P., *Les origines de la grande industrie allemande* (Paris, 1933).

Bergues, H. and others, *La prévention des naissances dans la famille. Ses origines dans les temps modernes* (Paris, 1960).

Blayo, C., 'La population des pays socialistes européens – II, Autres aspects de l'évolution', *Pop.* 21, no. 5 (1966), 971–1012.

244

Boserup, E., *The conditions of agricultural growth* (London, 1965).

Boulding, K. E., 'The Malthusian model as a general system', *Soc. & Ec. Stud.*, 4, no. 3 (1955), 195–205.

Bourgeois-Pichat, J., 'Les facteurs de la fécondité non dirigée', *Pop.*, 20, no. 3 (1965), 383–424.

Burn, R., *The ecclesiastical law*, 8th ed. corrected, 4 vols. (London, 1824).

Carr-Saunders, A. M., *The population problem* (Oxford, 1922).

Census of Ireland 1901, Parl. Papers, 1902, cxxix.

Census 1961, England and Wales, Fertility Tables (h.m.s.o., 1966).

Charles, E., 'The effect of present trends in fertility and mortality upon the future population of Great Britain and upon its age composition', in Hogben, L. (ed.), *Political arithmetic* (London, 1938), 73–105.

Chow, L. P., 'A programme to control fertility in Taiwan', *Pop. Stud.* xix, pt. 2 (1965), 155–66.

*Cipolla, C., *The economic history of world population* (London, 1962).

Clark, C. and Haswell, M., *The economics of subsistence agriculture*, 2nd ed. (London, 1966).

Coale, A. J., 'The effects of changes in mortality and fertility on age composition', *Milbank Mem. Fund. Qu.*, xxxiv, no. 1 (1956), 79–114.

Coale, A. J., 'The voluntary control of human fertility', *Proc. Am. Phil. Soc.*, 111, no. 3 (1967), 164–9.

*Coale, A. J. and Hoover, E. M., *Population growth and economic development in low-income countries* (Princeton, 1958).

Connell, K. H., *The population of Ireland 1750–1845* (Oxford, 1950)

Creighton, C. *History of epidemics in Britain*, 2 vols. (Cambridge, 1891 & 1894).

Dandekar, K., 'Vasectomy camps in Maharashtra', *Pop. Stud.*, xvii, pt. 2 (1963), 147–54.

Darwin, C., *On the origin of the species*, 5th ed. (London, 1869).

Darwin, C., *Essay of 1844*, in *Charles Darwin and Alfred Russel Wallace. Evolution by natural selection*, pub. for xv International Congress of Zoology and the Linnean Society of London (Cambridge, 1958).

*Davis, K. and Blake, J., 'Social structure and fertility: an analytic framework', *Ec. Dev. & Cult. Change*, 4, no. 3 (1956), 211–35.

Deane, P. and Cole, W. A., *British economic growth 1688–1959* (Cambridge, 1962).

Demos, J., 'Notes on life in Plymouth Colony', *W. & M. Qu.*, 3rd ser., 22 (1965), 264–86.

Deniel, E. and Henry, L., 'La population d'un village du Nord de la France, Sainghin-en-Mélantois, de 1665 à 1851', *Pop.*, 20, no. 4 (1965), 563–602.

Deprez, P., 'The demographic development of Flanders in the eighteenth century', in Glass, D.V. and Eversley, D.E.C. (eds.), *Population in history* (London, 1965).

Douglas, M., 'Population control in primitive groups', *Br. J. Sociol.*, XVII, no. 3 (1966), 263–73.

Drake, K.M., *Marriage and population growth in Norway 1735–1865*, unpub. Ph.D. thesis (Cambridge, 1964).

Drake, K.M., 'The growth of population in Norway 1735–1855', *Scand. Ec. Hist. Rev.*, XIII, no. 2 (1965), 97–142.

Drummond, J.C. and Wilbraham, A., *The Englishman's food*, revised ed. (London, 1958).

Durand, J.D., 'The modern expansion of world population', *Proc. Am. Phil. Soc.*, 111, no. 3 (1967), 136–59.

Eaton, J.W., and Mayer, A.J., 'The social biology of very high fertility among the Hutterites. The demography of a unique population'. *Hum. Biol.*, XXV, no. 3 (1953), 206–64.

Ensor, R.C.K., *England 1870–1914* (Oxford, 1936).

Farr, W., *Vital statistics* (London, 1885).

Fleury, M. and Henry, L., *Nouveau manuel de dépouillement et d'exploitation de l'état civil ancien* (Paris, 1965).

Fortes, M., 'A demographic field study in Ashanti', in Lorimer, F. and others, *Culture and human fertility* (Paris, 1954), 253–339.

Gautier, E. and Henry, L., *La population de Crulai* (Paris, 1958).

George, M.D., *London life in the eighteenth century* (London, 1930).

Gille, H., 'The demographic history of the northern European countries in the eighteenth century', *Pop. Stud.* III, pt. 1 (1949), 3–65.

Glass, D.V. (ed.), *Introduction to Malthus* (London, 1953).

*Glass, D.V. and Eversley, D.E.C. (eds.), *Population in history* (London, 1965).

Godwin, W., *Of population* (London, 1820).

*Goode, W.J., *World revolution and family patterns* (New York, 1963).

Goubert, P., 'En Beauvaisis: problèmes démographiques de XVIIᵉ siècle', *Annales*, 7, no. 4 (1952), 453–68.

*Goubert, P., *Beauvaisis et le Beauvaisis de 1600 a 1730*, 2 vols. (Paris, 1960).

Goubert, P., 'La mortalité en France sous l'ancien Régime. Problèmes et hypothèses', in *Problèmes de mortalité*, Actes du Colloque International de Démographie Historique, Liège 1963 (no pub. date), 79–92.

Graunt, J., *Natural and political observations*, in Hull, C.H. (ed.), *The economic writings of Sir William Petty*, 2 vols. (New York, 1963).

Griffith, G.T., *Population problems of the age of Malthus* (Cambridge, 1926).

Habakkuk, H.J., 'English population in the eighteenth century', *Ec. Hist. Rev.*, 2nd ser., VI, no. 2 (1953), 117–33.

Habakkuk, H.J., 'Family structure and economic change in nineteenth century Europe', in Bell, N.W., and Vogel, E.F. (eds.), *A modern introduction to the family* (New York, 1960), 163–72.

Hajnal, J., 'European marriage patterns in perspective', in Glass, D.V. and Eversley, D.E.C. (eds.), *Population in history* (London, 1965).

Hatt, P.K., *Background of human fertility in Puerto Rico* (Princeton, 1952).

*Hauser, P.H. and Duncan, O.D. (eds.), *The study of population. An inventory and appraisal* (Chicago, 1959).

Helleiner, K.P., 'New light on the history of urban populations', *J. Ec. Hist.*, XVIII, no. 1 (1958), 56–61.

Henripin, J., *La population canadienne au début du XVIIIe siècle* (Paris, 1954).

Henry, L., *Anciennes familles genevoises* (Paris, 1956).

Herlihy, D., 'Population, plague and social change in rural Pistoria 1201–1430, *Ec. Hist. Rev.*, 2nd ser., XVIII, no. 2 (1965), 225–44.

Himes, N.E., *Medical history of contraception* (Baltimore, 1936).

Hogben, L. (ed.), *Political arithmetic* (London, 1938)

Hollingsworth, T.H., 'The demography of the British peerage', supplement to *Pop. Stud.*, XVIII, no. 2 (1964).

John, A.H., 'Aspects of English economic growth in the first half of the eighteenth century', in Carus-Wilson, E.M. (ed.), *Essays in economic history*, vol. 2 (London, 1962).

Jutikkala, E., 'The great Finnish famine in 1696–7', *Scand. Ec. Hist. Rev.*, III, no. 1 (1955), 48–63.

Keynes, J.M., *The economic consequences of the Peace* (London, 1919).

Keynes, J.M., 'A reply to Sir William Beveridge', *Ec. J.*, XXXIII (1923), 476–86.

Krause, J.T., 'Some implications of recent work in historical demography', *Comp. Stud. Soc. & Hist.*, I, no. 2 (1959), 164–88.

Krzywicki, L., *Primitive society and its vital statistics* (London, 1934).

Lassen, A., 'The population of Denmark in 1660', *Scand. Ec. Hist. Rev.*, XIII, no. 1 (1965), 1–30.

Laslett, P., *The world we have lost* (London, 1965).

Leibenstein, H., *Economic backwardness and economic growth* (New York, 1963).

Leibenstein, H., 'Population growth and the take-off into sustained growth', in Rostow, W. W. (ed.), *The economics of take-off into sustained growth* (London, 1963).

Levasseur, E., *La population française*, 3 vols. (Paris, 1889–92).

Levy, M. J., 'Aspects of the analysis of family structure', in Coale, A. J., Fallers, L. A., Levy, M. J., Schneider, D. M., and Tomkins, S. S., *Aspects of the analysis of family structure* (Princeton, 1965)

Levy, M. J., and Westoff, C. F., 'Simulation of kinship systems', *New Scientist*, 27, no. 459 (1965), 571–2.

Lorimer, F. and others, *Culture and human fertility* (Paris, 1954).

McKeown, T. and Record, R. G., 'Reasons for the decline of mortality in England and Wales during the nineteenth century', *Pop. Stud.*, XVI, pt. 2 (1962), 94–122.

*Malthus, T. R., *First essay on population 1798*, Royal Economic Society reprint (London, 1926).

Mehlan, K. H., 'The Socialist countries of Europe', in *Family planning and population programs* (Chicago, 1966), 207–26.

Mitchell, B. R., and Deane, P., *Abstract of British historical statistics* (Cambridge, 1962).

Mols, R., *Introduction à la démographie historique des villes d'Europe du XIVe au XVIIIe siècle*, 3 vols. (Louvain, 1954–6).

Muramatsu, M., 'Japan', in *Family planning and population programs* (Chicago, 1966), 7–20.

Ohlin, G., 'Mortality, marriage and growth in pre-industrial populations', *Pop. Stud.*, XIV, pt. 3 (1961), 190–7.

*Petersen, W., *Population* (New York, 1961).

Potter, R. G., 'Birth intervals: structure and change', *Pop. Stud.* XVII, pt. 2 (1963), 156–66.

*Pressat, R., *L'analyse démographique* (Paris, 1961).

Pullan, B., 'The famine in Venice and the new Poor Law 1527–9, *Boll. Ist. Stor. Soc.*, V–VI, (1963–4), 141–202.

Rabel, G., *Kant*, (Oxford, 1963).

Razzell, P., 'Population change in eighteenth century England. A reinterpretation', *Ec. Hist. Rev.*, 2nd ser., XVIII, no. 2 (1965), 312–32.

Registrar-General, *Statistical Review of England and Wales* (H. M. S. O.).

248

*Reinhard, M.R. and Armengaud, A., *Histoire générale de la population mondiale* (Paris, 1961).

Rele, J.R., 'Some aspects of family and fertility in India', *Pop. Stud.* xv, pt. 3 (1962), 267–78.

Report from Mr. Finlaison, Actuary of the National Debt, on the evidence and elementary facts on which Tables of Life Annuities are founded, Parl. Papers, 1829, iii, 287–355.

Robinson, W.C., 'Urban-rural differences in Indian fertility', *Pop. Stud.* xiv, pt. 3 (1961), 218–34.

Rowntree, R.S, *Poverty: a study of town life* (London, 1901).

Royal Commission on Population, Papers of
  vol. i, Lewis-Faning, E., *Family limitation and its influence on human fertility during the past fifty years* (H.M.S.O., 1949)..
  vol. vi, Glass, D.V. and Grebenik, E., *The trend and pattern of fertility in Great Britain: a report on the family census of 1946* (H.M.S.O., 1954).

Russell, J.C., *British medieval population* (Albuquerque, 1948).

Ruwet, J., 'Crises de mortalité et mortalités de crise à Aix-la-Chapelle (xviie-début du xviiie siècle)', in *Problèmes de mortalité.* Actes du Colloque International de Démographie Historique, Liège, 1963 (no pub. date), 379–408.

*Sauvy, A., *Théorie générale de la population,* 2 vols. (Paris, 1952–4).

Sauvy, A. and others, *Le 'Tiers-Monde'* (Paris, 1961).

Short, T., *New observations on city, town and country bills of mortality* (London, 1750).

Sjoberg, G., *The preindustrial city* (New York, 1960).

Slicher van Bath, B.H., *The agrarian history of western Europe, A.D. 500–1850* (London, 1963).

Smith, A., *An inquiry into the nature and causes of the wealth of nations,* M'Culloch, J.R. (ed.), new ed. (Edinburgh, 1863).

Solow, R.M., 'Technical change and the aggregate production function', *Rev. Ec. & Stat.,* xxxix (1957), 312–20.

*Spengler, J.J. and Duncan, O.D. (eds.), *Demographic analysis* (Glencoe, 1956).

Statistik des Deutschen Reichs (Kaiserlichen statistischen Amt, Berlin).

Stone, L., 'Social mobility in England, 1500–1700', *P. & P.,* 33 (1966), 16–55.

Szabady, E., Tekse, K., Pressat, R., and Blayo, C., 'La population des pays socialistes européens – i, La fécondité', *Pop.,* 21, no. 5 (1966), 939–70.

Taeuber, I.B., *The changing population of Japan* (Princeton, 1958).

Taeuber, I. B., 'Japan's demographic transition re-examined', *Pop. Stud.* xiv, pt. 1 (1960), 28–39.

Thirsk, J., 'Industries in the countryside', in Fisher, F. J. (ed.), *Essays in the economic and social history of Tudor and Stuart England* (Cambridge, 1961).

Tooke, T., *A history of prices*, 4 vols. (London, 1838–48).

*United Nations, Department of Social Affairs, Population Division, Report 17, *The determinants and consequences of population trends* (New York, 1953).

United Nations, Department of Social Affairs, Population Division, Report 25, *Methods for population projections by sex and age* (New York, 1956).

United Nations, Department of Social Affairs, Population Division, Report 26, *The aging of populations and its economic and social implications* (New York, 1956).

United Nations, Department of Social Affairs, Population Division, Report 29, *Multilingual demographic dictionary* (New York, 1958).

Utterström, G., 'Some population problems in pre-industrial Sweden', *Scand. Ec. Hist. Rev.*, ii, no. 1 (1954), 103–65.

Utterström, G., 'Climatic fluctuations and population problems in early modern history', *Scand. Ec. Hist. Rev.*, iii, no. 1 (1955), 3–47.

Valmary, P., *Familles paysannes au XVIIIe siècle en Bas-Quercy* (Paris, 1965).

Watt, K. E. F., 'The effect of population density on fecundity in insects', *Can. Entom.*, xcii, no. 9 (1960), 674–95.

Weber, A. F., *The growth of cities in the nineteenth century* (New York, 1899).

Wilson, C., *England's apprenticeship 1603–1763* (London, 1965).

Wrigley, E. A., *Industrial growth and population change* (Cambridge, 1961).

Wrigley, E. A., 'The supply of raw materials in the industrial revolution', *Ec. Hist. Rev.*, 2nd ser., xv, no. 1 (1962), 1–16.

Wrigley, E. A., 'Family limitation in pre-industrial England', *Ec. Hist. Rev.*, 2nd ser., xix, no. 1 (1966), 82–109.

Wrigley, E. A. (ed.), *An introduction to English historical demography* (London, 1966).

Wrigley, E. A., 'A simple model of London's importance in changing English society and economy 1650–1750', *P. & P.*, 37 (1967), 44–70.

Wrigley, E. A., 'Mortality in pre-industrial England: the example of Colyton, Devon, over three centuries', *Daedalus*, vol. 97, no. 2 (1968), 246–80.

*Wynne-Edwards, V. C., *Animal dispersion in relation to social behaviour* (Edinburgh and London, 1962).

Index

250

Acknowledgments

Acknowledgment is due to the following for illustrations (the number refers to the page on which the illustration appears):
Frontispiece Deutsche Fotothek; 7 The Wellcome Foundation; 31 Axel Poignant; 61 Mansell Collection; 107, 145 British Museum; 203 Daily Telegraph.

The diagrams and maps were designed by John Messenger and drawn by John Messenger and Design Practitioners Ltd.

World University Library

Books published or in preparation

Economics and Social Studies

The World Cities
Peter Hall, *Reading*

The Economics of Underdeveloped Countries
Jagdish Bhagwati, *MIT*

Development Planning
Jan Tinbergen, *Rotterdam*

Human Communication
J. L. Aranguren, *Madrid*

Education in the Modern World
John Vaizey, *London*

Money
Roger Opie, *Oxford*

Soviet Economics
Michael Kaser, *Oxford*

Decisive Forces in World Economics
J. L. Sampedro, *Madrid*

Key Issues in Criminology
Roger Hood, *Durham*

The Sociology of Africa
Jacques Maquet, *Paris*

History

The Emergence of Greek Democracy
W. G. Forrest, *Oxford*

Muhammad and the Conquests of Islam
Francesco Gabrieli, *Rome*

The Civilisation of Charlemagne
Jacques Boussard, *Poitiers*

The Crusades
Geo Widengren, *Uppsala*

The Ottoman Empire
Halil Inalcik, *Ankara*

Humanism in the Renaissance
S. Dresden, *Leyden*

The Rise of Toleration
Henry Kamen, *Warwick*

The Scientific Revolution 1500-1700
Hugh Kearney, *Sussex*

The Left in Europe
David Caute, *London*

The Rise of the Working Class
Jürgen Kuczynski, *Berlin*

Chinese Communism
Robert C. North, *Stanford*

The Italian City Republics
Daniel Waley, *London*

The Culture of Japan
Mifune Okumura, *Kyoto*

The History of Persia
Jean Aubin, *Paris*

A Short History of China
G. F. Hudson, *Oxford*

The Arts

The Language of Modern Art
Ulf Linde, *Stockholm*

Twentieth Century Music
H. H. Stuckenschmidt, *Berlin*

Art Nouveau
S. Tschudi Madsen, *Oslo*

Palaeolithic Cave Art
P. J. Ucko and A. Rosenfeld, *London*

Primitive Art
Eike Haberland, *Mainz*

Expressionism
John Willett, *London*

Language and Literature

French Literature
Raymond Picard, *Paris*

**Russian Writers and Society
1825-1904**
Ronald Hingley, *Oxford*

Satire
Matthew Hodgart, *Sussex*

The Romantic Century
Robert Baldick, *Oxford*

Philosophy and Religion

Christian Monasticism
David Knowles, *London*

New Religions
Ernst Benz, *Marburg*

Sects
Bryan Wilson, *Oxford*

Earth Sciences and Astronomy

The Structure of the Universe
E. L. Schatzman, *Paris*

Climate and Weather
H. Flohn, *Bonn*

Anatomy of the Earth
André Cailleux, *Paris*

Zoology and Botany

Mimicry in Plants and Animals
Wolfgang Wickler, *Seewiesen*

Lower Animals
Martin Wells, *Cambridge*

The World of an Insect
Rémy Chauvin, *Strasbourg*

Plant Variation and Evolution
D. Briggs, *Glasgow*
S. M. Walters, *Cambridge*

The Age of the Dinosaurs
Björn Kurtén, *Helsinki*

Psychology and Human Biology

Eye and Brain
R. L. Gregory, *Edinburgh*

The Ear and the Brain
E. C. Carterette, *UCLA*

The Biology of Work
O. G. Edholm, *London*

The Heart
Donald Longmore, *London*

The Psychology of Fear and Stress
J. A. Gray, *Oxford*

The Tasks of Childhood
Philippe Muller, *Neuchâtel*

Doctor and Patient
P. Lain Entralgo, *Madrid*

Chinese Medicine
P. Huard and M. Wong, *Paris*

Physical Science and Mathematics

The Quest for Absolute Zero
K. Mendelssohn, *Oxford*

What is Light?
A. C. S. van Heel and
C. H. F. Velzel, *Eindhoven*

Mathematics Observed
Hans Freudenthal, *Utrecht*

Quanta
J. Andrade e Silva and G. Lochak, *Paris*
Introduction by Louis de Broglie

Applied Science

Words and Waves
A. H. W. Beck, *Cambridge*

The Science of Decision-making
A. Kaufmann, *Paris*

Bionics
Lucien Gérardin, *Paris*

Data Study
J. L. Jolley, *London*